Presenting English Grammar

The English Instructor's
Training and Reference
Handbook

With hundreds of example sentences with full
explanations and 62 illustrative tables

BY RICHARD E. McDORMAN

Introduction by **Maria Antonia Ospina**

Presenting English Grammar:
The English Instructor's Training and Reference Handbook

Copyright © 2004-2011 by Richard E. McDorman
Introduction copyright © 2011 by Richard E. McDorman
and Maria Antonia Ospina

All rights reserved.

ISBN 0983911258

Except for brief quotations used in reviews or academic use or citation, no part of this book may be reproduced by any means without the written permission of the publisher.

Cover artwork and design by
Alexandro J. Angelbello

TABLE OF CONTENTS

Introduction by Maria Antonia Ospina 7
Preface 9
Forward: A Grammatical Sketch of the English Language 13

Part 1: Presenting English Verbs 21
1.1 Verbal Tense and Aspect 21

    1.1.1 Overview of English verbal tense and aspect
    (*present, past,* and *future* tenses; *simple, perfect,* and *continuous* aspects) 21

    1.1.2 Present simple and present continuous 22

    1.1.3 Past continuous 23

    1.1.4 Past simple and present perfect 24

    1.1.5 Past simple and past perfect 25

    1.1.6 Future simple and related forms 26

    1.1.7 Future simple and future perfect 27

    1.1.8 Perfect continuous tenses 28

    1.1.9 Regular and irregular past simple forms 28

    1.1.10 Adverbial phrases of time with different tenses 30

1.2 Modal and auxiliary verbs 33

    1.2.1 Modal and non-modal auxiliary verbs 33

    1.2.2 Quasi-modal verbs 34

    1.2.3 The modal verbs *can* and *may* 35

    1.2.4 Common problems with modal verbs
    (*have to* and *must; ought to* and *should*) 35

    1.2.5 *To have* as an auxiliary and a main verb 36

    1.2.6 Auxiliary *do* 36

1.3 Conditional clauses 39

    1.3.1 The first conditional 39

1.3.2 The second conditional..40
1.3.3 The third conditional..41
1.3.4 The zero conditional..42
1.4 Verbs followed by infinitives and verbs followed by gerunds........................ 45
1.5 The subjunctive mood.. 47
1.6 Phrasal verbs.. 49
1.6.1 Phrasal verbs defined and explained...49
1.6.2 Separable and non-separable phrasal verbs 49
1.7 Contractions 53
1.7.1 Contracting *to be* and other auxiliary verbs with nouns and pronouns........53
1.7.2 Contracting auxiliary verbs with *not*..57

Part 2: Presenting English Nouns and Pronouns 59
2.1 Nouns and noun phrases.. 59
2.2 Definite and indefinite articles (*the* and *a/an*).. 61
2.3 Regular and irregular plural forms 63
2.4 Count and non-count nouns... 69
2.5 Collective nouns... 73
2.6 Pronouns... 75
2.6.1 Types of pronouns..75
2.6.2 Personal pronouns 77
2.6.3 Reflexive pronouns 79

Part 3: Presenting other Types of Words: Adjectives, Preposition, and Adverbs... 81
3.1 Adjectives and adjective phrases... 81
3.2 Placement of adjectives within the clause.. 83
3.3 Comparative and superlative forms of adjectives.. 85
3.3.1 Adjectives with irregular comparative and superlative forms 88
3.3.2 Using comparative and superlative forms of adjectives...............................89
3.4 Participles and gerunds 91
3.4.1 Present and past participles 91
3.4.2 Past participles and passive verbs..93

3.5 Prepositions and prepositional phrases 95
3.6 Preposition stranding in spoken English 97
3.7 Problems with the meaning of certain prepositions 101
3.8 Adverbs 105
3.9 Types of adverbs and the placement of adverbs within the clause 109
    3.9.1 Adverbs of manner, frequency, degree, place, and time 109
    3.9.2 Clause-final adverbs (*too*, *as well*, *either*, etc.) 113
3.10 Comparative and superlative forms of adverbs 115
3.11 Problems with the meaning of certain adverbs and adjectives 117
3.12 *No* and *not* 119

Part 4: Presenting English Syntax 123
4.1 An overview of English syntax 123
4.2 Question formation: subject-verb inversion 125
    4.2.1 Forming questions with auxiliary verbs 125
    4.2.2 Forming questions with negated auxiliary verbs 127
4.3 Forming questions with wh-words 129
4.4 Using question tags 133
4.5 Indirect (reported) questions 137
4.6 Regular word order (SVO) in declarative sentences 139
4.7 Impersonal clauses 141
    4.7.1. Impersonal *it* 141
    4.7.2. Impersonal *there* 143
4.8 Subject-verb inversion in declarative sentences 145
    4.8.1. Subject-verb inversion with initial negative
    adverbs and prepositional phrases 145
    4.8.2 Conditional clauses beginning with *were* and *had* 148
    4.8.3 Subject-verb inversion with initial adverbs and stative verbs 149
    4.8.4 Subject-verb inversion with *so* and *neither* 151
4.9 The emphatic *do* 151

Index of Tables 153

INTRODUCTION

Presenting English Grammar (PEG) is a handbook that should be in every English teacher's library, as well as a resource available in every academic institution. The grammar teacher will find in *PEG* a unique, well-written, comprehensive, and valuable resource. Teaching English grammar effectively is one of the most common and difficult challenges the English teacher will face. English teachers are confronted with a daunting amount of information, which makes it difficult to choose an effective method and user-friendly guide for teaching grammar. Fortunately, *PEG* is convenient one-stop shopping for teachers interested in presenting grammatical structures and syntax in a clear, efficient manner. McDorman presents dozens of different grammar structures that are all thoroughly explained in easy-to-understand language, making *PEG* an effective tool for the grammar teacher who is often faced with complex linguistic and grammatical terminology. *PEG* is also an excellent point of reference for ESL teachers seeking guidance on what to anticipate in the classroom and how to treat the unique learning needs of ESL students. It is for these reasons that *PEG* has become an invaluable tool in workshops and seminars designed to prepare teachers for the multiple challenges they will face in the classroom. My own experience conducting teacher training workshops and seminars has shown *PEG* to be especially effective in identifying potential grammatical pitfalls and teaching sticking points commonly encountered in the ESL classroom, as well as how to best meet those challenges. Both novice and experienced teachers alike have been enthusiastically receptive to the use of *PEG* in workshops because it identifies which structures are difficult to present and how best to explain them.

McDorman provides the grammar teacher with tested techniques that yield immediate results for the problems that many of us, as grammar teachers, have faced in our classrooms. Complex concepts are explained simply without over-simplification. PEG handles many of the challenging questions that teachers ask about presenting difficult material. All English and ESL teachers, whether at the secondary, adult education, or collegiate level, will benefit from McDorman's clear, analytical approach.

It is unusual to find a teacher training resource that so adeptly addresses the difficulties that confront our students. I have had the pleasure of working first-hand with the author and can assure my fellow English and ESL instructors that McDorman has presented a very effective manual for teaching the structure of English. PEG is a guide long overdue and a "must read" for all ESL teachers and anyone else who must present and understand English grammar.

Maria Antonia Ospina

PREFACE

The primary goal of this handbook is to familiarize adult English as a second language (adult ESL) instructors with the most important grammatical concepts and concomitant grammatical difficulties encountered by students in and out of the classroom while providing both novice and experienced instructors with the tools necessary to exemplify and explain, when necessary, such concepts in a clear and effective manner. By carefully reviewing the examples, explanations, and notes contained in this handbook, adult ESL instructors will learn to employ the so-called "natural" method (sometimes also referred to as the "direct" method) in their presentations of several of the most essential points of English grammar. While this handbook is not intended to provide an exhaustive review of English grammar, it does aim to address the most common sources of grammatical difficulty encountered by teachers and students in typical adult ESL settings. The examples presented throughout this handbook use Standard American English and cover a wide range of grammatical concepts at the beginning, intermediate, and advanced proficiency levels.

This work emphasizes practical *grammatical* concepts, that is, issues mainly involving English morphology and syntax, along with some important lexical issues. Matters entirely related to pronunciation (i.e., phonetics and phonology) are for the most part not taken up in this manual. Upon completing their review of the material presented in this handbook, ESL instructors should be able to apply the natural method to their presentations of the most fundamental grammatical topics encountered in the classroom, across the proficiency levels and independent of theme-specific lesson content. Although this handbook does not presuppose any specific linguistic training on the part of the reader and technical linguistic jargon has been intentionally kept to a minimum, some basic linguistic terminology has been used out of necessity given the content of this work. Readers who are unfamiliar with basic linguistic concepts (such as *morphology*, *syntax*, *lexicon*, *aspect*, *grammaticality*, etc.) should be able to consult standard reference materials in order to resolve their uncertainties with a minimum of difficulty.

The author has developed and revised this handbook over the course of many years of training novice and experienced instructors to teach a broad range of ESL curricula (including general, academic, and business English at all proficiency levels) to adult learners in diverse educational settings and instructional formats (such as private, one-on-one tutorials and multi-level intensive English programs taught in small and medium-sized groups). Each grammatical concept presented in this handbook is accompanied by numerous examples of realistic usage to aid the reader in understanding those concepts and to assist the instructor with his or her presentation of those grammatical concepts in the classroom. Finally, the reader should keep in mind that this handbook is *practical* rather than theoretical in nature and has been specifically designed to serve as a useful addition to the ESL instructor's professional "tool kit." It is the author's hope that the reader will find this handbook to be easily approachable and highly relevant to the issues encountered during his or her daily instructional responsibilities.

Note on grammaticality tables and symbols used

Many of the grammatical concepts presented in this handbook are illustrated with examples of grammatical and ungrammatical usage. Such examples frequently appear in *grammaticality tables* that judge whether the example sentences conform to the grammatical principles of Standard American English. Three symbols are used in these tables:

X	To indicate that the example sentence is clearly ungrammatical.
√	To indicate that the example sentence is clearly grammatical.
?	To indicate that the example sentence is of questionable or unclear grammaticality or meaning.

Examples:

?	I don't know	**about what**	you're talking.	
√	I don't know	**what**	you're talking	**about.**
X	I don't know		you're talking	**about.**

In addition, in accordance with standard linguistic practice, the asterisk (*) is used before ungrammatical sentences or forms wherever they appear in the text. Example: * *I don't know nobody.*

A GRAMMATICAL SKETCH OF THE ENGLISH LANGUAGE

English is an Indo-European language, ultimately related to most of the languages of Europe (the primary exceptions being Basque, Finnish, Estonian, Hungarian, and ancient Etruscan) and many languages spoken in central and southern Asia. More specifically, English is a West Germanic language, descended from the Anglo-Saxon dialects first brought to Britain in the fifth through seventh centuries AD from the European continent. Although English is closely related to other West Germanic languages, such as Dutch, Frisian, and German, the structure and vocabulary of Modern English have diverged substantially from those of its sister tongues, mainly owing to repeated contacts between speakers of English and speakers of other languages, primarily Old Norse and Middle French, from the eighth through fourteenth centuries AD. In large part as a result of its contact with Middle French from c. 1100-1400 AD, English has acquired a vast number of loanwords of ultimately Latin origin. Most English words that end in –ity, -tion, -ous, -ism, and -tic, for example, have similar cognates in the Romance languages, a fact that your Spanish, Portuguese, and French-speaking students should find helpful in their language studies.

Although earlier stages of English, particularly Old English, had fairly complicated verbal systems, the modern English verb is simple in its morphology (that is, in its total number of conjugated forms). Most English verbs have no more than five distinct forms. For example, the "regular" verb *to walk* can be conjugated as follows: *walk, walks, walking,* and *walked*; the "irregular" verb *to eat* is only slightly more complex: *eat, eats, eating, ate,* and *eaten*. Notwithstanding the fact that the

English verb is less complicated in its conjugated forms than the verbs of most Romance (and indeed most other European) languages, experience has taught us that this lack of formal complexity is of little help to most of our students, for what English lacks in morphological complexity, it makes up for in its very complicated *syntax*—the rules and principles related to the correct ordering of words and phrases in a sentence.

Most verb forms in English are analytical (or periphrastic)—they involve more than one word. Although English verbs lack a large number of distinct conjugated forms, the English *verb phrase* relies on the use of auxiliary verbs to impart grammatical meaning. This fact of English grammar has posed seemingly endless problems to learners for two principal reasons. First, English depends heavily on the use of a special class of verbs known as *modal auxiliaries* (e.g., *will, would, shall, should, can, could, may, might, must, ought to*) to express fine shades of mood and aspect; the native languages of many if not most of our students lack this special type of verb and instead express such meaning by modifying the verbal root in some way, usually through suffixation. Many English students are uncomfortable with the concept of modal verbs and may hesitate to use them, and it will be your job to help them overcome this barrier to effective communication in English.

In addition to the modal auxiliary verbs, English also makes use of the non-modal auxiliary verbs *to do, to have,* and *to be* in a number of the language's most important verbal constructions, such as questions and negated verbs, and the perfect and continuous "tenses." Students frequently confuse these auxiliary verbs (especially *to do* and *to be*) and are often unsure of their correct usage. The second reason that the analytical English verb poses a difficulty to students involves the strict ordering of words in the English sentence. Unlike many other languages (such as Spanish and Russian), English demands strict adherence to the formulaic word order subject-verb-object (or **SVO**) in most constructions, with the important exception of interrogative clauses. In the few exceptions to the SVO rule in non-interrogative sentences, the verb is almost always the second element in the sentence. Moreover, within the verb phrase itself each element must be strictly ordered. Most ESL students will find sentences such as *I would have never gone skiing if I had known that it was going to rain* barely comprehensible at first. However, once you have mastered teaching English using the natural method, you should be able to guide your students with confidence to eventual mastery of even the most complicated English verbal constructions.

An additional complication to the English verbal system is the complex system of negation that began to evolve in the late sixteenth century. Unlike the methods of negation utilized in the Romance languages, Modern English grammar usually requires that an *auxiliary verb* be placed before the negative adverb *not*, with contraction common in spoken English. Thus, early Modern English **They knew him not* has been replaced with *They didn't know him*, and the eloquent but archaic-sounding *Ask not what your country can do for you* would normally be rendered as *Don't ask what your country can do for you* in everyday spoken English.

The English noun phrase is morphologically simple compared to the English verb; nevertheless, students typically find difficulty in correctly using possessive and plural forms. For example, the vast majority of English nouns form their plural by adding what is written as *–s* or *–es* to the singular form. However, depending on the final **sound** of the singular noun, this plural ending may be pronounced in one of three ways: as [s], [z], or [Iz]. In addition to the regular formation of plurals, a handful of nouns have retained vestiges of the original Old English strong inflection in which the vowel of the monosyllabic stem is modified (e.g., singular *tooth* but plural *teeth*; singular *man* but plural *men*). Although this method of pluralization once characterized a certain class of Old English nouns, most such nouns have become regular through the forces of analogy. It should be noted that some nouns, such as the names of scientific disciplines and certain diseases, usually lack plural forms (e.g., *physics, home economics, geology;* the *mumps, beriberi, rickets*). Moreover, certain nouns are singular in form but plural in function (e.g., *people, the government*). In addition to pluralization, all nouns can be inflected for the possessive case by adding what is written as *'s*. Like the pluralizing suffix, this morpheme is realized phonetically as either [s], [z], or [Iz] depending on the last **sound** of the noun to which it is affixed.

The Modern English pronominal system is perhaps the most morphologically complex component of English grammar. The personal pronouns have retained their ancient forms that are inflected for case; that is, their forms differ according to their syntactic function in the clause. Thus, when used as a subject or predicate nominative, the first person singular pronoun is *I*; when used as an object of a verb or preposition, or when used in a syntactically ambiguous context, the first person singular pronoun is realized as *me*. Finally, when used in the possessive case, the same pronoun is realized as either *my* or *mine*, depending on whether the word is placed before (*my*) or after (*mine*) the noun or noun phrase to which it pertains. The Modern English system of personal pronouns is remarkable in that it fails to distinguish the second person singular and plural pronouns; thus, sentences such as *Are you coming to dinner?* are semantically ambiguous in that the number of the subject is unclear. As many native speakers of English are aware, the current personal pronoun system is something of a novelty; as recently as three hundred fifty years ago, a sizeable number of English speakers still observed a regular distinction between singular *thou* (which is etymologically related to Spanish *tú*, French *tu* and German *Du*) and plural *ye* or *you*. Today, a very small minority of English speakers living in isolated communities of eastern North America still makes a distinction between the singular *thou* and the plural *you*.

Although the English adjective is unremarkable from a broad linguistic perspective, its use is often a matter of substantial difficulty for ESL students. In terms of its syntax, the adjective is usually placed directly before the noun or noun phrase that it modifies, a deviation from the pattern found in most Romance languages, whose speakers typically prefer that the adjective be placed after the noun; nevertheless, Romance speakers tolerate a substantial number of exceptions to this general rule. When it comes to mastering the use of English adjectives, students often find learning comparative and superlative adjectival forms to be a difficult task. Because English employs two different methods of forming comparatives and superlatives, some students (and a few instructors) mistakenly believe that they must memorize which adjectives belong to which category. In truth, however, the comparative and superlative forms of almost all adjectives are entirely predictable based on the *number of syllables* comprising the adjective in question. In general, the comparative form of an adjective of one or two syllables is created by adding the suffix –*er*, and the superlative form is created by adding the suffix –*est* (e.g., *greener, greenest; happier, happiest*). In similar fashion, the comparative form of an adjective of three or more syllables is created by placing the adverb *more* before the adjective, and its superlative form is created by preposing the adverb *most* (e.g., *more beautiful, most beautiful; more independent, most independent*). Exceptions to this rule only occur when adding the suffixes –*er* or –*est* to an adjective would result in an odd or difficult pronunciation, technically known as phonotactic awkwardness (e.g., *more willing, most willing*, not **willinger, *willingest; more sprung, most sprung*, not **sprunger, sprungest*). It should be pointed out, however, that in everyday spoken English it is becoming increasingly common for speakers to use *more* and *most* to form the comparative and superlative of many one and two syllable adjectives, even where Standard English requires forms with –*er* and –*est* (e.g., *Orlando is a lot more fun than Tallahassee, She's the most humble person I know*).

English prepositional phrases display one highly unusual and for many students somewhat troubling feature: unlike the prepositions of almost all other languages that actually have them (not all languages actually have prepositions), English prepositions do not always require that their object be placed directly after them, at least in the spoken form of the language. This phenomenon, known as preposition stranding, results in the deletion of the relative pronoun that was the original object of the preposition and movement of the preposition to the end of the clause in declarative sentences and preservation of the relative pronoun with movement of the preposition to clause-final position in interrogative sentences. Thus, instead of *She is the woman about whom I am talking* (which some speakers still prefer in written English), spoken English prefers *She's the woman I'm talking about*. Similarly, the sentence *That's the house I grew up in* is the spoken English equivalent of the more formal written version *That is the house in which I grew up*. In questions, preposition movement strands the preposition without deletion of the relative pronoun object, as in *What are you talking about?* and *Which store did you say you live next to?* Although a few prescriptive grammarians still exhort their students to use the more contrived (and linguistically questionable) versions *About what are you talking? And Next to which store did you say you live?*, such constructions are rare in spoken English.

The English adverbial phrase is in most respects a simple construction. The derivation of adverbs from adjectives normally takes place with the simple addition of the adverbializing suffix –ly, although numerous exceptions to this general pattern exist (e.g., *fast*, not **fastly*; *in a green manner*, not **greenly*). Some participles may also participate in this process (e.g., *embarrassingly, decidedly*). Syntactically, adverbs tend to present greater difficulties to learners than do adjectives, since the correct ordering of adverbs among clausal constituents is often lexically determined; that is, certain adverbs or classes of adverbs must be placed in specific positions in the clause. For example, the adverbs *too*, *as well*, and *either* must be placed in clause-final position. On the other hand, certain adverbs of time and manner (e.g., *often, sometimes, frequently, never, always, usually,* etc.) are usually placed before the last verb of the verb phrase, unless the verb is *to be*, in which case such adverbs immediately follow the verb. Most of the remaining adverb-related complications (from the students' perspectives) involve the meaning of specific adverbs, such as the subtle differences among *very, so,* and *too,* and the seemingly intractable confusion between *no*, which is an adjective, and the adverb *not*.

Without question the most complex aspect of English grammar is its syntax. Ultimately derived from the ancient Greek συντασσειν (*syntassein*), or "to put in order," *syntax* refers to the rules or principles whereby words or other elements of sentence structure are combined to form grammatical sentences. The *typical* default syntax of the English declarative sentence is subject-verb-object (often abbreviated as **SVO**) and unlike many other languages (numbering in the thousands), non-imperative English sentences must always contain an overt subject. However, the actual linguistic situation is far more complex. In fact, one of the fundamental principles of English syntax is that, with few exceptions, the verb must be the second fundamental constituent of a declarative sentence. The truth of this statement is born out in syntactically complex sentences such as *Under no circumstances will I eat broccoli, There are two and a half million people in Miami, Under this tombstone rests the body of poor old Jesse James,* and *Rarely has it rained this much in July*. Although we may instruct our students that each of these examples is the result of **subject-verb inversion**—a sound practice for teaching students correct English syntax without hopelessly confusing them—instructors should be aware that a more complex process is at work. For example, we teach our students that when forming questions, we must first use an *auxiliary verb* and then perform subject-verb inversion, as in *Why did you eat my slice of the pizza?* and *Haven't you* *always loved Paris in the springtime?* However, the actual rules are slightly different. Sentences of both types (*Under no circumstances will I eat broccoli* and *Why did you eat my slice of the pizza?*) are manifestations of the same phenomenon: when the subject is not the first fundamental constituent of the sentence, an *auxiliary* verb or a *stative* verb (a special verb that expresses state, location, or condition) must occupy the second constituent slot. This principle also conveniently explains why embedded questions—relative clauses that begin with wh-words—do not undergo subject-verb inversion (i.e., *I know where you live* and not **I know where do you live* or **I know where live you*).

Part 1: Presenting English Verbs

1.1 VERBAL TENSE AND ASPECT

1.1.1 Overview of English verbal tense and aspect

Various forms of the English verb explicitly indicate **tense**, or the *time* when the verbal action takes place, and **aspect**, or the *manner* in which the verbal action occurs. From a strict morphological perspective, English has only two tenses (*present* and *past*, or *past* and *non-past*, depending on one's theoretical leanings). However, these tenses can be combined with four aspects (simple, continuous, perfect, and perfect continuous) and with the modal verb *will*. The resulting combined forms of **tense** and **aspect** are traditionally referred to simply as **tenses**. The following table outlines the English system of verbal tense and aspect.

TABLE 1. SUMMARY OF ENGLISH VERBAL TENSE AND ASPECT

FUTURE **SIMPLE**	FUTURE **CONTINUOUS**	FUTURE **PERFECT**	FUTURE **PERFECT CONTINUOUS**
PRESENT **SIMPLE**	PRESENT **CONTINUOUS**	PRESENT **PERFECT**	PRESENT **PERFECT CONTINUOUS**
PAST **SIMPLE**	PAST **CONTINUOUS**	PAST **PERFECT**	PAST **PERFECT CONTINUOUS**

As you can see, English verbal *tenses* and *aspects* combine to form complex verb forms. The following table illustrates this system for the verb *to do*.

TABLE 2. CONJUGATED FORMS OF THE VERB *TO DO*

will do	will be doing	will have done	will have been doing
do(es)	am/is/are doing	have/has done	have/has been doing
did	was/were doing	had done	had been doing

Students typically encounter two primary difficulties in their attempts to master this system: learning the forms themselves and learning how to use the forms correctly. The following discussion describes how to effectively present English verbal forms and how to explain and exemplify their correct usage.

1.1.2 Present simple and present continuous

The **present simple** tense expresses habits and habitual truths—actions that always or never take place. It is important for both the instructor and student to understand that in most instances (the main exception being verbs of sensation, as in *I smell something burning* or *I hear what you're saying*), this tense is **not** used to indicate that the verbal action is taking place at the moment of speech. For example, in the sentences *I **eat** breakfast every morning*, *My mother **speaks** Chinese*, and *They never **go** to the movies on Fridays*, the verb is conjugated in the **present simple** tense. For most verbs (the exceptions are *to be* and *to have*), the **present simple** is formed by using the infinitive without *to* (a form known as the **verbal stem**). The **present simple** forms of the third person singular (he, she, and it) add –**s** or –**es** to the verbal stem (e.g., *does, speaks, goes*). On the other hand, the **present continuous** tense is formed by using the appropriate **present simple** form of *to be* followed by the **present participle**. This tense is used when the action occurs at the moment of speech and is often accompanied by an adverbial phrase of time:

Right now I **am eating** breakfast, At this very moment they **are parking** the car, and It **is raining** cats and dogs outside. The **present continuous** tense is also used for actions that will take place imminently or soon in the future: We **are leaving** tomorrow, That show **is airing** again on Friday.

TABLE 3. PRESENT SIMPLE OF THE VERB TO GO

I **go**	we **go**
you **go**	you **go**
he, she, it **goes**	they **go**

1.1.3 Past continuous

The **past continuous** tense is formed by using the appropriate **past simple** form of to be followed by the **present participle**. This tense is used to express an action that was in progress (and not finished) at a time in the past, and is often used to report an action that was in progress at a particular time in the past: Maria said that she **was eating** dinner last night at Pizza Hut, and I told you that I **was playing** basketball last night. This tense is also used to describe a situation that took place over a period of time in the past: It **was raining** for six hours yesterday. The **past continuous** tense is also used to describe a state, event, or action that was planned in the past: We **were going** to take a vacation, but we didn't have enough money, and John had known for many months that he **was dying** of cancer. In addition, the **past continuous** tense is used for past actions that were interrupted or already in progress at a given time in the past: What **was** your sister **doing** at ten o'clock last night?; I **was sleeping** when the phone rang; and When Kennedy was shot, my grandmother **was watching** television.

TABLE 4. PRESENT, PAST, AND FUTURE CONTINUOUS OF THE VERB *TO GO*

I **am/was/will be going**	we **are/were/will be going**
you **are/were/will be going**	you **are/were/will be going**
he, she, it **is/was/will be going**	they **are/were/will be going**

1.1.4 Past simple and present perfect

The **past simple** (sometimes called the "simple past") tense is used to express that the verbal action began and ended in the past: *Yesterday I **went** to bed at six o'clock*; *In 1971, the Pittsburgh Pirates **won** the World Series*; *I **walked** to work this morning*. The **present perfect** tense is used to indicate that the verbal action began in the past and either has not yet ended, or has ended but has some relevance for the present; this tense is often used to talk about experiences, changes, and continuing situations: *This week I **have gone** to bed at six o'clock every night*; *So far this season, the Pittsburgh Pirates **have won** twenty games*; *I **have walked** to work three times this month*. The form of the verb in the **past simple** tense depends on the particular verb involved, as English has two classes of verbs: those that form the **past simple** tense by adding what is usually written as *–ed* to the verbal stem, and those that form the **past simple** tense in some other way (usually by changing the stem vowel or by adding a suffix other than *–ed*, or both). The **present perfect** tense is formed by using the appropriate present simple form of the verb *to have* followed by the **past participle** of the verb in question. In many circumstances, an adverb may be placed between the present tense form of *to have* and the past participle (e.g., *I **have never gone** to a Major League baseball game*).

TABLE 5. PAST SIMPLE OF THE VERB *TO GO*

I **went**	we **went**
you **went**	you **went**
he, she, it **went**	they **went**

TABLE 6. PRESENT PERFECT OF THE VERB *TO GO*

I **have gone**	we **have gone**
you **have gone**	you **have gone**
he, she, it **has gone**	they **have gone**

Students are sometimes confused by the use of these two tenses. In presenting the differences between the **past simple** and the **present perfect** tenses, it is helpful to use timelines to clarify the relative time periods involved in each tense (i.e., to demonstrate that the **past simple** begins and ends in the past, but that the **present perfect** begins in the past but may have not yet ended).

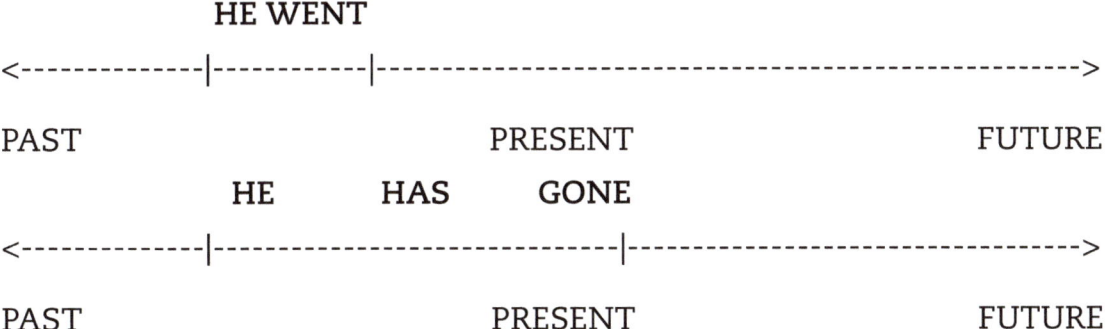

1.1.5 Past simple and past perfect

As explained above, the **past simple** tense is used to express that the verbal action began and ended in the past. The **past perfect** tense, however, is used to express that one action began in the past *before* another past action. The **past perfect** tense is formed by using the appropriate **past tense** form of the verb *to have* followed by the past participle. Although many sentences with verbs conjugated in the **past perfect** tense contain clauses with another verb conjugated in the **past simple** (e.g., *I **had** already **gone** to bed when the phone **rang***), such a clause is not required, so long as the past action before which the verb conjugated in the **past perfect** tense is implied or understood (e.g., *I **had** not **seen** the flag of Iraq before the Persian Gulf War*).

TABLE 7. PAST PERFECT OF THE VERB *TO GO*

I had gone	we had gone
you had gone	you had gone
he, she, it had gone	they had gone

1.1.6 Future simple and related forms

The **future simple** of *all* verbs is formed simply by adding the modal verb **will** before the infinitive without *to* (e.g., *I **will eat** lunch at noon, He **will** not **win** a gold medal*). In the past, some grammarians preferred that the modal verb **shall** be used for the first person, singular and plural, in the **future simple** tense (e.g., *I **shall go** to London on Thursday, We **shall visit** Paris in the springtime*). However, very few native speakers of English still observe this point of grammar. In addition to the **future simple**, which conveys a vague sense of certainty to native speakers, future actions can also be expressed by using the phrase **to be going to** before the verb in question (e.g., *I **am going to** go to London on Thursday, We **are going to** visit*

Paris in the springtime). This method of indicating future action feels less formal and less certain to native speakers.

TABLE 8. FUTURE SIMPLE OF THE VERB *TO GO*

I **will go**	we **will go**
you **will go**	you **will go**
he, she, it **will go**	they **will go**

1.1.7 Future simple and future perfect

Again, the **future simple** tense is used to express that the verbal action will begin at some point in time after the moment of speech. In contrast, the **future perfect** tense is used to express that one action will begin *in the future* before another (future) action. The **future perfect** tense is formed by using the **future tense** form of the verb *to have* (i.e., **will have**) followed by the past participle. Unlike those with verbs conjugated in the **past perfect** tense, many sentences with verbs conjugated in the **future perfect** contain clauses with another verb conjugated in the **present simple** tense preceded by an adverb or adverbial phrase of time (e.g., *I **will have** already **gone** to bed **when** the phone **rings***). Analogous to constructions involving the **past perfect** tense, such clauses are not required, so long as the future action before which the verb conjugated in the **future perfect** tense is implied or understood (e.g., *I **will** not **have seen** the flag of Iraq until my upcoming trip to the Middle East*).

TABLE 9. FUTURE PERFECT OF THE VERB *TO GO*

I **will have gone**	we **will have gone**
you **will have gone**	you **will have gone**
he, she, it **will have gone**	they **will have gone**

1.1.8 Perfect continuous tenses

The **present, past,** and **future perfect** tenses may be combined with the **continuous** aspect to create compound tenses, as described in **Table 1** above. In each case, the past participle of the verb *to be* (**been**) plus the *present participle* follow the appropriately tensed form of the verb *to have*. Examples: *I* **have been working** *on an important project; Before I started my new book, I* **had been working** *on an important project; By this time tomorrow, I* **will have been working** *on an important project*. The **present perfect continuous** tense is used to indicate that the verbal action was continuous in the recent past and continues up to the present; it indicates actions that occurred continuously in the recent past (e.g., *My shoes are dirty because I* **have been cutting** *the grass; I* **have** *recently* **been eating** *a low carbohydrate diet*). The **past perfect continuous** tense is used to indicate that the verbal action began in the past before another past event and persisted over a period of time (e.g., *I* **had been eating** *a lot of chocolate when my doctor ordered me to stop; Johanna* **had been wandering** *around New York City for an hour before she hailed a taxicab*). Similarly, the **future perfect continuous** tense is used to indicate that the verbal action will begin in the future before another future event and will continue over a period of time (e.g., *By this time next year, you* **will have been working** *at the restaurant for five years*).

TABLE 10. PRESENT, PAST, AND FUTURE PERFECT CONTINUOUS OF THE VERB *TO GO*

I **have/had/will have been going**	we **have/had/will have been going**
you **have/had/will have been going**	you **have/had/will have been going**
he **has/had/will have been going**	they **have/had/will have been going**

1.1.9 Regular and irregular past simple forms

When it comes to the **past simple** tense, English verbs come in two varieties: those whose **past simple** is formed by adding a dental suffix ([t], [d], or [Id]) that is usually written as *–ed* or *–d* to the verbal stem (i.e., the infinitive without *to*), and those whose **past simple** is formed in some other way. Verbs whose **past simple** is formed by adding the suffix *–ed* or *–d* to the verbal stem are normally referred to as *regular verbs*, whereas verbs whose **past simple** is formed in other ways are referred to as *irregular verbs*.

The **past simple** of an *irregular verb* is generally formed in one of three ways: by changing the stem vowel—most irregular verbs consist of only a single syllable (e.g., *run*, **ran**; *sing*, **sang**; *read*, **read**), by changing the stem vowel and adding an irregular suffix (e.g., *bring*, **brought**; *seek*, **sought**), or by not changing anything at all (*put*, **put**; *hit*, **hit**; *bid*, **bid**). Only a few irregular verbs fail to conform to one of these three patterns (notable examples include *to be*, *to go*, and *to have*). Although irregular verbs are not *entirely* irregular (most can be classified as belonging to a certain subclass and conforming to certain patterns), they must nevertheless be learned individually by students. Most irregular verbs also have irregular **past participles**, which must also be memorized.

TABLE 11. IRREGULAR VERB PATTERNS

Vowel alternation (to *sing*, to *win*, to *run*, to *read*, to *fight*, to *write*, to *fly*, etc.)

I, you, he... **sing(s)**	I, you, he... **sang**
I, you, he...**win(s)**	I, you, he... **won**
I, you, he... **run(s)**	I, you, he... **ran**
I, you, he... **read(s)**	I, you, he... **read**
I, you, he... **fight(s)**	I, you, he... **fought**
I, you, he...**write(s)**	I, you, he...**wrote**
I, you, he... **fly(ies)**	I, you, he...**flew**
I, you, he... **eat(s)**	I, you, he...**ate**
I, you, he... **sit(s)**	I, you, he...**sat**

Vowel alternation plus suffix (*to bring, to think, to buy, to seek, to teach, etc.*)

I, you, he... **bring(s)**	I, you, he... **brought**
I, you, he...**think(s)**	I, you, he... **thought**
I, you, he... **buy(s)**	I, you, he... **bought**
I, you, he... **seek(s)**	I, you, he... **sought**
I, you, he... **teach(es)**	I, you, he... **taught**

No change (*to bid, to hit, to put, etc.*)

I, you, he... **bid(s)**	I, you, he ... **bid**
I, you, he... **hit(s)**	I, you, he... **hit**
I, you, he... **put(s)**	I, you, he... **put**

1.1.10 Adverbial phrases of time with different tenses

It is common in English to use *adverbial phrases of time* to reinforce or specify the time period during which an action takes place. By using such *time phrases*, you can **exemplify rather than explain** the meaning and usage of English verbal tenses. For example, we commonly use phrases such as *all the time, always, usually, every day*, and other such adverbial phrases to indicate that the verbal action takes place *habitually* in tandem with the **present simple** tense (e.g., *I **usually walk** to work on Thursdays, You **play** golf **all the time**, My uncle **goes** to the gym **every day***).

By contrasting these phrases with those that indicate that the verbal action is taking place at the moment of speech, such as *right now, at the moment,* and *at this very second*, for example, you can guide the student to an understanding of the differences between the **present simple** and **present continuous** tenses (e.g., *I **teach** English **every day**, but I **am teaching** a class **right now**; Carlos **normally** eats lunch at*

1:00, but **right now** *he* **is eating** *at noon*). Other such adverbial phrases of time can help clarify the usage of other tenses (*tomorrow, next month, in the future*, with the **future simple** tense, for example; and *ago, last night/week/month/year, yesterday, in a given year*, with the **past simple** tense). Finally, it is important that students understand that the **future simple** tense is *never* used after adverbial phrases of time, a point of grammar that differs from many other languages. Thus, the sentence *I will have arrived* **by the time** *you* **get** *home* is grammatical, whereas the sentence **I will have arrived* **by the time** *you* **will get** *home* is not.

1.2 MODAL AND AUXILIARY VERBS

1.2.1 Modal and non-modal auxiliary verbs

Whereas many other languages, including all of the Romance languages, make heavy use of suffixation to mark verbs for time, mood, aspect, and the like, English relies primarily on a special class of verbs called *auxiliary* verbs to impart grammatical meaning. English has two varieties of auxiliary verbs: modal auxiliaries and non-modal auxiliaries. The **non-modal auxiliary** verbs are *to be, to have,* and *to do.* These verbs function as other normal verbs do, and are inflected for person in the present tense and for tense in the past, although all three verbs have irregular past tense forms. When used as auxiliary verbs, the verb *to be* is followed by the present participle (e.g., *John **is singing** in the choir on Friday*), *to have* is followed by the past participle (e.g., *John **has sung** in the choir for five years*), and *to do* is followed by the verbal stem (e.g., *John **does sing** in the choir—it's true!*).

Modal auxiliary verbs are a special class of verbs that are different from other, normal verbs. First, modal auxiliary verbs are not inflected for person or tense. Thus, modal auxiliary verbs have the same first, second, and third person singular forms (e.g., *I **can**, you **can**, he **can**—not *he **cans***). Furthermore, although we divide modal auxiliary verbs into "present" and "past" tense forms for convenience and for historical reasons, modal auxiliary verbs really do not have any tense at all. For example, the modal auxiliary verb **could** can be used to refer to present, past, or future actions (e.g., *When I was a child, I **could** climb a tree in one minute; Right now I am so hungry I **could** eat a horse; When you come to work tomorrow, **could** you please arrive an hour early?*). However, when the verbal action refers to the past, only the *past* forms may be used (e.g., *When I was a child, I **could** climb a tree in one minute* is possible, whereas **When I was a child, I **can** climb a tree...* is not).

TABLE 12. MODAL AUXILIARY VERBS

"Present" forms	"Past" forms
will	would
can	could
shall	should
may	might
must	
ought to	
had better	

Modal auxiliary verbs express differences in the speaker's *mood* (thus, the name *modal* auxiliary verbs) toward the main verb. Thus, *He **will** go* expresses that the speaker believes that the verbal action will take place in the future and is definite; *he **can** go* expresses that the speaker believes that the verbal action is possible (in the sense that the subject has the ability to perform the verbal action), but not definite; *he **may** go* expresses that the speaker believes that the verbal action is possible (in the sense that circumstances may permit the verbal action to take place), but not definite; *he **must** go* expresses that the speaker believes that the verbal action is imperative, and so forth.

1.2.2 Quasi-modal verbs

English has two quasi-modal verbs: **ought to** and **had better**, which function as modal verbs in all respects, but do not follow the regular pattern of the form of modal verbs. Whereas all other modal verbs are comprised of only one word, these two modal verbs are comprised of two words that function as a single unit. Both **ought to** and **had better** are used to indicate that the speaker believes that the subject should carry out the verbal action. The quasi-modal verb **ought to** is roughly synonymous with **should** (e.g., *I* **should** *leave now* and *I* **ought to** *leave now* are close in meaning). The quasi-modal verb **had better** is a stronger form of **ought to**, and is used to indicate that if the verbal action is not carried out, negative consequences are likely to follow (e.g., *I* **had better** *leave now; if I don't, I might get hurt*).

1.2.3 The modal verbs *can* and *may*

The modal verbs **can** and **may** are both used to express that the verbal action is possible, but they do so with different implications. The modal verb **can** is used to express that the subject has the actual ability to perform the verbal action (e.g., *I* **can** *speak French because I was born in France, I* **can** *play the piano because I took piano lessons for twelve years*). On the other hand, the modal verb **may** is used to express that the subject has the ability to perform the verbal action but will do so only if he or she chooses, or if circumstances permit it (e.g., *I* **may** *go to France next week if I have the time, I* **may** *play the piano if my fingers don't hurt*).

1.2.4 Common problems with auxiliary and modal verbs

Students often encounter difficulties distinguishing the meanings of certain auxiliary and modal verbs. For example, students may be unsure as to when to use **have to** and when to use **must** to indicate that the verbal action is imperative (e.g., what is the difference in meaning between *I* **have to** *go now* and *I* **must** *go now?*). In general, **must** is more urgent and imperative than **have to**, and is used in situations of greater necessity. Another source of confusion for students in the difference in meaning between **should** and **ought to** (for example, is there any difference in meaning between *I* **should** *go now* and *I* **ought to** *go now?*). The modal verb **ought to** is used to indicate obligation or duty (*You ought to work harder than that*), advisability or prudence (*You ought to wear a raincoat*), desirably (*You ought to have been there; it was great fun*), or probability (*She ought to finish by next week*), Like **ought to**, **should** is also used to express obligation or duty (*You should send her a note*) and probability (*They should arrive at noon*); however, **should** is also used to express conditionality or contingency (*If she should fall, I would catch her*) and to moderate the directness or bluntness of a statement (*I should think he would like to go*), although this use is quickly becoming archaic.

1.2.5 *To have* as an auxiliary and as a main verb

The verb **to have** may be used as either an auxiliary verb (*I* **have** *already* **eaten** *lunch*) or as a main verb (*I* **have** *laryngitis*). When used as an auxiliary verb, **to have** behaves like *to do* and *to be* in terms of contraction and its use in questions. Thus, *I* **have** *already* **eaten** *lunch* can be contracted to *I've already* **eaten** *lunch*, and when one is questioned **Have** *you already* **eaten** *lunch*, he or she may answer *Yes, I* **have**. However, when **to have** is used as a main verb, it cannot function as an auxiliary verb; that is, it does not contract with the pronoun subject or with the adverb *not* (*I* **have** *laryngitis, not *I've laryngitis; I don't* **have** *laryngitis, not *I* **have**n't *laryngitis*) and cannot be used alone to answer a question. Thus, the answer to the question *Do you* **have** *laryngitis* is *Yes, I* **do**, and not **Yes, I* **have** or **Yes, I've*.

1.2.6 The auxiliary verb *to do*

The auxiliary verb **to do** is one of the greatest complexities of English verbal syntax, and its mastery is a source of great difficulty for our students. Its use is mandatory in questions and negative constructions that do not otherwise need or use an auxiliary verb, and it can be used to emphasize the truth of a statement. In questions that do not otherwise have an auxiliary verb, the verb **to do** must precede the subject, even when the main verb is **to do** (**Do** *you* **like** *Chinese food?*, not **Like you Chinese food?*; **Did** *you* **do** *anything last night?*, not **Did you anything last night?*). Similarly, in negative constructions that do not otherwise have an auxiliary verb, the verb **to do** must precede the adverb *not* before the main verb (*I* **do** *not* **like** *Chinese food*, not **I not like Chinese food*). Finally, the auxiliary verb **to do** may be used before the main verb to emphasize the truthfulness of the statement (*I* **do** *really* **love** *Chinese food*; *When I was a child, I* **did** *eat a lot of junk food*).

1.3 CONDITIONAL CLAUSES

English uses four types of conditional constructions to indicate the result of a certain condition or conditions. Note that in all conditional clauses in which the result clause follows the condition clause, use of the conjunction *then* is optional. All conditional constructions follow a similar patt

| IF | **CLAUSE 1** (CONDITION CLAUSE) | THEN | **CLAUSE 2** (RESULT CLAUSE) |

Note, however, that in conditional constructions, either clause may come first. However, if the *result* clause comes first, the conjunction *then* is not used:

| **CLAUSE 1** (RESULT CLAUSE) | IF | **CLAUSE 2** (CONDITION CLAUSE) |

1.3.1 The first conditional

The **first conditional** is used when talking about the future to indicate the result of a particular condition or situation. In the **first conditional**, the verb in the *condition* clause is in the **present simple** tense, while the verb in the *result* clause is in the **future simple** tense (*If it **rains** tomorrow, then I **will stay** home*). In this construction, there is a real possibility that the condition will happen. The **first conditional** is used when we are thinking about a possible future condition and the result that will take place if that condition occurs.

TABLE 13. THE FIRST CONDITIONAL

If	Condition	(then)	Result
If	it **rains** tomorrow,	(then)	I **will stay** home.
If	I **win** the lottery,	(then)	I **will buy** a new car.
If	you **leave** early,		where **will** you **go**?
If	my brother **calls**,	(then)	I **won't** talk to him.
If	I **am** hungry,	(then)	I **will** eat a sandwich.

1.3.2 The second conditional

The **second conditional** is like the first conditional in that we use it when talking about the future; when we use the **second conditional**, we are thinking about a particular condition in the future and the result of this condition. However, unlike the first conditional, the **second conditional** is used when there is **not** a real possibility that the condition will happen. The **second conditional** is used to express an unreal possibility or a dream. In the **second conditional**, the verb in the *condition* clause is in the **past simple** tense, while the verb in the *result* clause uses **would** or **could** plus the base verb (*If I **won** the lottery, I **would buy** a new car*). The important thing about the **second conditional** is that there is an unreal possibility that the condition will happen.

TABLE 14. THE SECOND CONDITIONAL

If	Condition	(then)	Result
If	it **rained** tomorrow,	(then)	I **would stay** home.
If	I **won** the lottery,	(then)	I **would buy** a new car.
If	you **left** early,		where **would** you **go**?
If	you **had** a car,	(then)	you **could** drive to work.
If	my brother **called**,	(then)	I **wouldn't** talk to him.
If	she **spoke** French,	(then)	she **could** live in France.
If	I **were** hungry,	(then)	I **would** eat a sandwich.

Notice that for the **second conditional**, when the verb in the *condition* clause is **to be**, it is always conjugated **were** (*If he **were** hungry, then he **would eat** a sandwich; If I **were** you, I **wouldn't do** that*). This is a special form of the verb known as the *subjunctive mood* that today is used mainly in conditional clauses.

1.3.3 The third conditional

While the first and second conditionals are used talk about the future, the **third conditional** is used to talk about the past. The **third conditional** is used to discuss a condition in the past that did *not* happen; therefore, there is no possibility for this condition. The **third conditional** is also like a dream, but with *no possibility of the dream coming true*. In the **third conditional**, the verb in the *condition* clause is in the **past perfect** tense, while the verb in the *result* clause uses *would have* (or *might/could have*) plus the past participle (*If I **had won** the lottery, I **would have bought** a new car*); we use the **past perfect** tense to talk about the impossible past condition. The important thing about the **third conditional** is that both the *condition* and the *result* are impossible now.

TABLE 15. THE THIRD CONDITIONAL

If	Condition	(then)	Result
If	it **had rained** yesterday,	(then)	I **would have stayed** home.
If	I **had won** the lottery,	(then)	I **would have bought** a new car.
If	they **hadn't done** that,	(then)	we **might have** won the game.
If	You **had left** early,		where **would** you **have gone**?
If	Mr. Mason **had called**,	(then)	you **could have** talked to him.
If	my brother **had called**,	(then)	I **wouldn't have talked** to him.
If	I **had been** hungry,	(then)	I **would have eaten** a sandwich.

1.3.4 The zero conditional

Finally, we use the so-called **zero conditional** when the result of the conditional clause is always true, as in laws of nature or scientific facts. In the **zero conditional**, the result of the condition is an absolute certainty. When we use this conditional clause, we are not thinking about the present, past, or future, but rather of simple facts. In the **zero conditional**, both the *condition* and the *result* are in the **present simple** tense because they are *always* true. The important thing about the **zero conditional** is that it always has the same result.

TABLE 16. THE ZERO CONDITIONAL

If	Condition	(then)	Result
If	water **gets** too hot,	(then)	it **boils**.
If	you **guess** all six numbers,	(then)	you **win** the lottery.
If	I **am** late for work,	(then)	my boss **gets** angry.
If	ice **reaches** 33 degrees,		**does** it **melt**?
If	you **drink** spoiled milk,	(then)	you **become** sick.

1.4 VERBS FOLLOWED BY INFINITIVES AND VERBS FOLLOWED BY GERUNDS

In English, one verb is often used after another verb. Sometimes the second verb is in the **infinitive** form (*I **need to sleep**, they **want to go** home*), and sometimes the second verb is in the **gerund** form (*I dislike **sleeping**, they considered **staying** at home for Christmas*). **Gerund** is the grammatical term for the present participle when used as a noun. Whether a verb is followed by the **infinitive** or the **gerund** is determined lexically; that is, it is not entirely predictable and must be learned by memory. Some verbs can be followed by either the **infinitive** or the **gerund** without much change in meaning (*I **like to play** golf* or *I **like playing** golf, It **started to snow*** or *It **started snowing***). However, some verbs can be followed by either the **infinitive** or the **gerund**, but the two forms have different meanings; for these verbs, when the **infinitive** follows the verb, the meaning is directed toward the present or the future, whereas when the **gerund** follows, the meaning is directed toward the past (*I **regret to inform** you that you were not selected*, but *I **regret informing** him of my decision because afterwards he became angry and stormed out of the room*). The following table lists some common verbs and the categories to which they belong.

TABLE 17. COMMON VERBS FOLLOWED BY GERUNDS AND INFINITIVES

Gerunds (always)	Infinitives (always)	Either (no change in meaning)	Either (change in meaning)
avoid	hope	begin	forget
enjoy	expect	cease	remember
dislike	want	continue	regret
finish	need	intend	purpose
mention	desire	start	propose
practice	demand	hate	try
miss		love	stop
suggest		advise	see
many phrasal verbs		like	hear
		permit	watch

1.5 THE SUBJUNCTIVE MOOD

The term **subjunctive mood** refers to a more formal, somewhat literary form of the verb not frequently used in casual English. Nevertheless, this verb form is still a part of English grammar and must be learned by advanced students. With the exception of the past tense form of the verb *to be*, the **subjunctive** only differs from the indicative (i.e., normal) form of the verb for the third person singular in the **present simple** tense. The form of the **subjunctive** is the same as the base form of the verb for all persons; as a result, the third person singular form of the **present simple** tense in the **subjunctive mood** lacks the characteristic suffix *–s/–es*. The **subjunctive** form of the verb is used in relative clauses that follow verbs or verb phrases of command, suggestion, urging, and the like: *I **demand** that he **leave** at once, We **suggest** that you **save** more money* (notice that there is no difference between the subjunctive and indicative form of the verb), *It **is imperative** that he not **get** caught*. The **past subjunctive** is used after the conjunction *if* and only differs from the indicative form of the verb for *to be*, in which case the form is ***were*** for all persons: *If I **were** you, I wouldn't do that; If he **were** a wealthier man he could buy a new car; If I **had** the chance, I would go* (notice that there is no difference between the past subjunctive and past indicative forms for verbs other than *to be*).

1.6 PHRASAL VERBS

1.6.1 Phrasal verbs defined and explained

Phrasal verbs are part of a large group of English verbs that are composed of more than one word. Most phrasal verbs are made up of a single-word verb (i.e., *to look*) and an adverbial particle (i.e., *after*), that when taken together function *as a single verb* (i.e., *to look after*). Thus, **phrasal verbs** are *multi-word* verbs that typically have a different meaning than the single-word verb on which the phrasal verb is based (*to look after* means *to care for* or *to take care of*, whereas *to look* means something entirely different). For students, learning the meaning of phrasal verbs is not particularly difficult, as this process is not much different from learning the meaning of single-word verbs.

1.6.2 Separable and non-separable phrasal verbs

The more difficult aspect of **phrasal verbs** involves learning how different phrasal verbs deal with objects. Transitive **phrasal verbs** (i.e., those that must take a direct object) often (but not always) separate their two parts by inserting the direct object noun between the base verb and the adverbial particle. This separation is usually optional when the direct object is a noun or a noun phrase; however, it is generally considered more formal to place the noun or noun phrase direct object after the entire **phrasal verb.** These phrasal verbs are known as **separable phrasal verbs.**

√	They	**looked**		**up**	the number.
√	They	**looked**	the number	**up.**	
√	John	**picked**		**up**	the groceries.
√	John	**picked**	the groceries	**up.**	
√	I	**will look**		**over**	the numbers.
√	I	**will look**	the numbers	**over.**	
√	My boss	**turned**		**down**	my offer.
√	My boss	**turned**	my offer	**down.**	

However, if the direct object is a *pronoun*, there is no choice but to separate the phrasal verb and insert the pronoun between the two parts.

X	They	**looked**		**up**	it.
√	They	**looked**	it	**up.**	
X	John	**picked**		**up**	them.
√	John	**picked**	them	**up.**	
X	I	**will look**		**over**	these.
√	I	**will look**	these	**over.**	
X	My boss	**turned**		**down**	it.
√	My boss	**turned**	it	**down.**	

On the other hand, some **phrasal verbs** function more like a verb plus a preposition, and since all prepositions must have an object, these **phrasal verbs** do not allow the object to separate the two parts of the phrasal verb, even if the object is a pronoun. These phrasal verbs are known as **inseparable phrasal verbs** or prepositional verbs.

X	They	**looked**	him	**after.**	
√	They	**looked**		**after**	him.
X	John	**picked**	them	**on.**	
√	John	**picked**		**on**	them.
X	I	**will wait**	her	**for.**	
√	I	**will wait**		**for**	her.
X	My boss	**talked**	me	**about.**	
√	My boss	**talked**		**about**	me.

1.7 CONTRACTIONS

In everyday spoken English, forms of the verb *to be* and a few other auxiliary verbs are often **contracted** with their subjects and with the adverb *not*. In this process, the subject and the auxiliary verb, or the auxiliary verb and the adverb *not* fuse to become a single word. Subject pronouns typically **contract** with present tense forms of the verb *to be*, present and simple past tense forms of the verb *to have*, and the modal auxiliary verbs *will* and *would*. In addition, singular nouns can contract with **is** and **has**.

1.7.1 Contracting *to be* and other auxiliary verbs with nouns and pronouns

TABLE 18. CONTRACTIONS WITH PRONOUNS AND PRESENT TENSE FORMS OF THE VERB *TO BE*

Subject	Verb	→	Contraction
I	am	→	I'm
you	are	→	you're
he	is	→	he's
she	is	→	she's
it	is	→	it's
noun	is	→	noun's
we	are	→	we're
they	are	→	they're

TABLE 19. CONTRACTIONS WITH PRONOUNS AND PRESENT TENSE FORMS OF THE VERB *TO HAVE*

Subject	Verb	→	Contraction
I	have	→	I've
you	have	→	you've
he	has	→	he's
she	has	→	she's
it	has	→	it's
we	have	→	we've
they	have	→	they've

TABLE 20. CONTRACTIONS WITH PRONOUNS AND PAST TENSE FORMS OF THE VERB *TO HAVE*

Subject	Verb	→	Contraction
I	had	→	I'd
you	had	→	you'd
he	had	→	he'd
she	had	→	she'd
it	had	→	it'd
we	had	→	we'd
they	had	→	they'd

TABLE 21. CONTRACTIONS WITH PRONOUNS AND THE VERB *WILL*

Subject	Verb	→	Contraction
I	will	→	I'll
you	will	→	you'll
he	will	→	he'll
she	will	→	she'll
it	will	→	it'll
we	will	→	we'll
they	will	→	they'll

TABLE 22. CONTRACTIONS WITH PRONOUNS AND THE VERB *WOULD*

Subject	Verb	→	Contraction
I	would	→	I'd
you	would	→	you'd
he	would	→	he'd
she	would	→	she'd
it	would	→	it'd
we	would	→	we'd
they	would	→	they'd

Note that the contracted forms of **it would, it had**, and **it will** are generally not used in writing. Also note that **contractions** with *would* and *had* are identical for all forms. Although this may at first cause some confusion for students, the context in which the forms appear will always resolve any questions, since *would* is always followed by the base form of the verb (i.e., the infinitive without *to*), whereas *had* is always followed by the **past participle**: *I'd [would] help you if I could*, but *I'd [had] helped you even before you asked*. A similar situation occurs with contractions involving the third person singular pronouns (and nouns) with *is* and *has*. Again, the context should resolve any ambiguities, since *has* must be followed by the **past participle** and *is* must be followed by the **present participle**: *She's [is] working right now*, but *She's [has] worked there for three years*.

X	They've	three children.
√	They have	three children.
X	John's	a nice wife.
√	John has	a nice wife.
√	They've seen	his three children.
√	John's talked to	your wife.
√	My mother's been	to South America twice.

It is important to note that the verb *to have* only contracts when it is used as an auxiliary verb, and never contracts when it is used as the main verb. Also, **contractions** are not possible when the subject and auxiliary verb are used to answer a question if the main verb is omitted

X	Q: Have you been to Mexico?	A: Yes, I've.
√	Q: Have you been to Mexico?	A: Yes, I have.
X	Q: Will you eat breakfast tomorrow?	A: Yes, I'll.
√	Q: Will you eat breakfast tomorrow?	A: Yes, I will.
X	Q: Are you Swedish?	A: Yes, I'm.

√	Q: Are you Swedish?	A: Yes, I am.
X	Q: Has she left yet?	A: Yes, she's.
√	Q: Has she left yet?	A: Yes, she has.

1.7.2 Contracting auxiliary verbs with *not*

In addition to contractions involving pronouns and auxiliary verbs, auxiliary verbs and the verb *to be* often contract with the adverb *not*. For most forms, the contraction is formed by deleting the vowel in *not* and suffixing the remaining *n't* to the auxiliary verb.

TABLE 23. CONTRACTIONS WITH PRESENT AND PAST TENSE FORMS OF THE VERB *TO BE* AND *NOT*

Verb	not	→	Contraction
am	not	→	*no contraction in Standard English*
are	not	→	aren't
is	not	→	isn't
was	not	→	wasn't
were	not	→	weren't

In Standard English, the first person singular present tense form of *to be* (i.e., *am*) cannot contract with *not*. However, you should be prepared to answer students' questions regarding the often-heard form *ain't*. Although this word is used as a contraction for *am* plus *not* in many English dialects (and is also sometimes used instead of *aren't* and *isn't*), this form is generally considered substandard and students should take care to avoid using it.

TABLE 24. CONTRACTIONS WITH AUXILIARY VERBS AND *NOT*

Verb	not	→	Contraction
do	not	→	don't
does	not	→	doesn't
did	not	→	didn't
has	not	→	hasn't
have	not	→	haven't
will	not	→	won't
would	not	→	wouldn't
shall	not	→	shan't
should	not	→	shouldn't
cannot	see note	→	can't
could	not	→	couldn't
may	not	→	none
might	not	→	mightn't
must	not	→	mustn't
ought	not	→	oughtn't

It should be noted that the contracted forms *mightn't* and *oughtn't* are uncommon in Standard English, and that the contracted form *shan't* is becoming obsolete; so in general, these forms should not be taught to students. In writing, *can* plus *not* is always written as one word, *cannot*, and never as two words (i.e., *can not*).

Part 2: Presenting English Nouns and Pronouns

2.1 NOUNS AND NOUN PHRASES

The English noun phrase is much simpler than the English verb phrase, all things considered, and students generally find that mastering English nouns is an easier proposition than mastering English verbs. Most English nouns have two **numbers** (singular and plural), although some nouns exist only in the singular (e.g., *physics*, *the flu*, *geology*) or the plural (e.g., *people*), and grammatical **gender** (that is, a system of grammatically marked noun classes) no longer exists in English. Furthermore, most English nouns form their plural by adding what is written as either **–s** or **–es** (and pronounced as either [s], [z], or [Iz]), although again some exceptions do exist. For most students, mastering the use of English personal pronouns is somewhat more difficult, if only for the reason that the English pronominal system is usually somewhat different than the pronominal system of the student's native language; however, the English pronominal system is not inherently complicated when compared to many other related languages (such as Latin, Greek, Irish, Russian, or German).

2.2 DEFINITE AND INDEFINITE ARTICLES

English has a **definite article** (*the*) and an **indefinite article** (*a/an*), both of which are used before noun phrases in certain situations. The **definite article** (*the*) can be used before both singular and plural nouns, but the **indefinite article** (*a/an*) can only be used before singular nouns. The **definite article** (*the*) is used to restrict the meaning of a noun or noun phrase to something that is known by both the speaker and the listener (*My mother went to* **the store**), to refer back to something that has already been mentioned (*There's a word for that. Now, what's* **the word***?*), or to refer to a group or a thing in general (**The English** *founded the American colonies,* **The light bulb** *has changed the world*). However, when a noun or noun phrase is used to refer to a group or class of things in general and is in the plural, the **definite article** is *not* used (**Light bulbs** *have changed the world*, not *****The light bulbs** *have changed the world*). When a noun is used in a non-defined or generalizing context, the **definite article** is not needed (*Time is money, Love is eternal*). So when a particular noun is used in an undefined context the **definite article** is not used, but when that same noun becomes defined, the **definite article** becomes mandatory (*I like* **whisky**, *but I don't like* **the whiskey** *you bought;* **Air** *is essential for life, but* **the air** *in Los Angeles is dangerous to breathe*). Also, the **definite article** is never used before the names of languages or scientific/academic disciplines (**English** *is a difficult language,* not *****The English** *is a difficult language; The English in fact refers to the inhabitants of England;* **Math** *is hard, but* **physics** *is harder,* not *****The math** *is hard but* **the physics** *is harder*—such a statement actually refers to some specific mathematical calculations and physical formulae).

The **indefinite article** *a/an* is used before a singular noun when the speaker refers to a noun that is one of many (*I met* **a friend** *for dinner last night*), that is any example of the class or type of thing to which the speaker refers (*Alice saw **a movie** about Thomas Jefferson*), or is meant to refer to a thing in general (***An apple** a day keeps the doctor away*). The important thing about the use of the **indefinite article** is that it is used before nouns when the speaker does not wish to refer to a specific or previously referred to noun, but to a noun in general (e.g., *I talked to **a doctor** about my skin condition, but not to **the doctor** you recommended*). While the **indefinite article** does not have a plural form, the adjectival determiner *some* can be used in a similar way before plural nouns (e.g., *I talked to **some doctors** about my skin condition, but not to **the doctors** you recommended*). Finally, the **indefinite article** has two forms: *a* and *an*. The **indefinite article** *a* is used before nouns and noun phrases that begin with a consonant *sound*, and the **indefinite article** *an* is used before nouns and noun phrases that begin with a vowel *sound*. Note that the spelling of the noun is irrelevant; it is the actual *pronunciation* that determines which **indefinite article** is used.

I met	***a friend***	for dinner.
I met	***an old friend***	for dinner.
I met	***an acquaintance***	for dinner.
I bought	***a house***	in that neighborhood.
I bought	***a yellow house***	in that neighborhood.
I have	***an hour***	to spend at the gym.
I have	***a horse***	at my father's farm.

2.3 REGULAR AND IRREGULAR PLURAL FORMS

Most English nouns form their plural by simply adding a suffix that is written as **s** or **es** to the singular noun; the plural suffix is usually written as **es** when the noun ends in the vowel /o/ (e.g., *potatoes, tomatoes, grottoes, indigoes*) or a sibilant (an s-like sound) (e.g., *passes, flashes, boxes, glasses*). These nouns are referred to as **regular nouns**. However, the way in which the plural suffix is *pronounced* depends on the final sound of the noun to which it is added. When the noun ends in a voiceless consonant (i.e., one whose articulation does not involve vibration of the vocal cords), the plural suffix is usually pronounced [s]. When the noun ends in a voiced consonant or a vowel (both of whose articulation requires vibration of the vocal cords), the plural suffix is pronounced [z]. Finally, when the noun ends in a sibilant, the plural suffix is pronounced [Iz]. However, when you present this information to your students, you should avoid technical terms like *voiced*, *voiceless*, and *sibilant* and instead rely on *examples* to successfully guide your students to the practice and production phases.

TABLE 25. PRONUNCIATION OF THE PLURAL SUFFIX –S/-ES

After voiceless consonant: [s]	After voiced consonant: [z]	After vowel: [z]	After sibilant: [Iz]
maps	tabs	gallows	masses
hats	lids	flaws	houses
packs	bags	rays	raises
giraffes	raves	brews	flashes
paths	lathes	boughs	garages
chips	malls	cows	lodges
huts	cars	mews	pages
rakes	hens	bows	misses
laughs	rams	sees	mazes
pups	fangs	ties	foxes

Although still considered **regular**, many nouns that end in [θ] (a voiceless *th* sound, as in *bath* and *path*) and [f] (as in *leaf* and *dwarf*) form their plurals by causing their final (voiceless) consonants to become voiced. Thus, final [θ] becomes [ð] (*baths* and *paths*), and final [f] becomes [v] (*leaves* and *dwarves*). Note the change in spelling for nouns that end in [f]. For some nouns that end in [θ], this change is optional (thus, some speakers pronounce *paths* as [pʰæθs] while others pronounce it as [pʰæːðz]).

In addition to **regular nouns**, English has two small classes of nouns that form their plurals in other ways. The first group of **irregular nouns** has been inherited from Old English and is a relic of earlier methods of pluralization that once were more widespread but have since been swept away by the regularizing forces of analogy (Old English possessed several distinct classes of nouns that formed their plurals in different ways, much as Modern German nouns do today). Most such nouns form their plurals by either changing their stem vowel or by not changing at all.

TABLE 26. NOUNS WITH IRREGULAR GERMANIC PLURAL FORMS

Singular form	Plural form	Method of pluralization
tooth	teeth	vowel change
foot	feet	vowel change
goose	geese	vowel change
louse	lice	vowel change
mouse	mice	vowel change
man	men	vowel change
woman	women	vowel change
child	children	irregular suffix
ox	oxen	irregular suffix
brother	brethren (note)	irregular suffix
sheep	sheep	no change
deer	deer	no change
moose	moose	no change
fish	fish/fishes	no change

Note: The noun *brother* has two plurals: the common plural is the regularly formed *brothers*; however, when the noun *brother* has the meaning 'one who shares a common ancestry, allegiance, character, or purpose with another or others,' the older plural *brethren* is often used, particularly in religious contexts.

The second group of **irregular nouns** is a more recent addition to the English language and represents borrowings from classical languages. English has borrowed many words from ancient Latin and Greek, which did not pluralize their nouns in the same way as English does. For many such borrowings, Modern English uses the original ancient Latin or Greek plural forms. For Latin nouns that end in *–um*, the plural is formed by changing the –*um* to –*a*; for Latin nouns that end in –*us*, the plural is formed by changing the –*us* to –*i*; for Latin nouns that end in –*a*, the plural is formed by changing the –*a* to –*ae*; for Latin nouns that end in –*ex* or –*ix*, the plural is formed by changing the –*ex* or –*ix* to –*ices*; and for Latin nouns that end in –*is*, the plural is formed by changing the –*is* to –*es*. For Greek nouns that end in –*on*, the plural is formed by changing the –*on* to –*a*. The table below exemplifies this process with some of the more common nouns of this class.

TABLE 27. NOUNS WITH IRREGULAR LATIN OR GREEK PLURAL FORMS

Singular form	Plural form	Method of pluralization
datum	data	–um to –a
rostrum	rostra	–um to –a
agendum	agenda	–um to –a
medium	media	–um to –a
cactus	cacti	–us to –i
alumnus	alumni	–us to –i
octopus	octopi	–us to –i
alga	algae	–a to –ae
alumna	alumnae	–a to –ae
crisis	crises	–is to –es
thesis	theses	–is to –es
apex	apices	–ex to –ices
appendix	appendices	–ix to –ices
criterion	criteria	–on to –a
etymon	etyma	–on to –a

Although English uses the classical plural forms for many nouns that have been borrowed from Latin and Greek, not all such nouns behave in this way. Nouns that have been part of the English lexicon for a longer period of time and nouns that have become extremely common tend to regularize their plural forms. Thus, the common plural form of *stadium* is *stadiums*, not *stadia*; and the common plural form of *arena* is *arenas*, not *arenae*. Similarly, the plural of the Greek loanword *pentagon* is *pentagons*, not the original *pentaga*. In teaching your students the irregular plural forms of words such as *criterion* and *apex*, the better practice is to present this group as a special class of nouns whose plurals must be memorized, not as a hard-and-fast rule to be applied across the board.

2.4 COUNT AND NON-COUNT NOUNS

Most English nouns can be divided into two broad categories: **count nouns**, which can be made plural and are countable (e.g., *car, man, street, candy bar*), and **non-count nouns**, which cannot be counted and usually have no plural (e.g., *love, heartache, coffee, trouble, peace*). **Count** and **non-count nouns** also differ in their article usage and in the adjectives that are used to modify them. When a **count noun** is singular and indefinite, the indefinite article *a/an* is used with it. On the other hand, **non-count nouns** are usually things that cannot be itemized or counted (such as *rice* or *water*), or abstract concepts (such as *remorse* or *ecstasy*). Such nouns most often have a singular form, but when they are indefinite, either the word *some* or nothing at all is used instead of the indefinite article.

How can one tell whether a noun is a **count noun** or a **non-count noun**? In most cases, a noun's status can be determined simply by thinking about its meaning. **Count nouns** are usually objects that can easily be counted, whereas **non-count nouns** are often substances that cannot be individually counted, or are large, abstract ideas. The following chart illustrates this concept.

TABLE 28. COUNT NOUNS AND NON-COUNT NOUNS

Count nouns: things that can be individually counted	Non-count nouns: abstract and uncountable
car	education
foot	soap
stadium	clothing
table	grass
examination	literature
error	empathy
answer	amazement
idea	happiness
telephone	water

Count nouns can be individually counted (*I bought **three hats***), while **non-count nouns** cannot (**I bought **three clothings***). When we need to indicate a certain quantity of a **non- count** substance (these nouns are sometimes referred to as *mass nouns*), we usually use a *quantifier* followed by the preposition *of* (*I bought **two pieces of new clothing**, Please bring us **four glasses of water**, John would like to borrow **a cup of sugar***). **Count nouns** and **non-count nouns** also differ in that different adjectives are used to modify them. The adjectives *many* and *few* are used to modify **count nouns**, whereas the adjectives *much* (or *a lot of*) and *little* are used to modify **non-count nouns**.

Subject	Verb	Adjective	Count noun	Non-count noun
My friend	has	**many**	cars.	
My friend	has	**a lot of (much)**		patience.
Mr. Smith	has	**few**	friends.	
Mr. Smith	has	**little**		patience.
John	owns	**many**	pieces of	clothing.
John	likes	**few**	varieties of	wine.
Your aunt	knows	**many**	people.	
Your aunt	shows	**much (a lot of)**		love.
Your aunt	shows	**little**		love.

2.5 COLLECTIVE NOUNS

A **collective noun** is a noun that denotes a collection of persons or things that is regarded as a single unit. In American English, when a **collective noun** refers to a group of things as whole, a *singular verb* is used. In British English and more formal American usage, some **collective nouns** (e.g., *government* or *committee*) take *plural verbs*. Collective nouns are often **uncountable** (and are therefore considered **non-count nouns**). The following are some examples of **collective nouns**.

TABLE 29. EXAMPLES OF COLLECTIVE NOUNS

People	Animals	Things
army	colony	bunch
audience	flock	bundle
band	gaggle	clump
class	herd	cookware
committee	pack	crockery
family	pod	furniture
gang	pride	pair
government	school	regalia
jury	swarm	set
orchestra		stack
people		group
police		
public		
staff		
trio		

Note that the **collective nouns** *people* and *police* always require a plural verb, and the **collective nouns** *staff, committee,* and *government* often takes a plural verb. Also, as you can see from the list above, **collective nouns** that denote people are the most common type of **collective noun**.

2.6 PRONOUNS

2.6.1 Types of pronouns

A **pronoun** is a word that substitutes for a noun or a noun phrase and designates persons or things asked for, previously specified, or understood from the context. The previously specified someone or something to which a pronoun refers is known as its *antecedent*. **Pronouns** are a diverse group of words and include a number of different subtypes: personal, demonstrative, indefinite, relative, reflexive/intensive, interrogative, and reciprocal **pronouns** can all 'stand in for' a noun or noun phrase. Examples of the different types of **pronouns** are displayed in the following table.

TABLE 30. EXAMPLES OF PRONOUN SUBTYPES

Personal	Demonstrative	Indefinite	Relative
I, me	this	everyone	who, whom
you	these	anyone	which
he, him	that	someone	that
she, her	those	everybody	whoever, whomever
it	such	anybody	whatever
we, us		somebody	whichever
they, them		all	whosoever, whomsoever
my, mine		any	whatsoever
your, yours		each	what
his		every	
her, hers		some	
its		none	
our, ours		one	
their, theirs		either	
		neither	

Reflexive	Interrogative	Reciprocal
myself	what	each other
yourself	who, whom	one another
himself	which	
herself		
itself		
ourselves		
yourselves		
themselves		
oneself		

2.6.2 Personal pronouns

Unlike English nouns, which usually do not change form according to how they are used in the sentence (with the exception of the addition of an –s ending to create the plural or other, irregular pluralizing mechanisms, or the *apostrophe + s* to create the possessive), **personal pronouns** change forms according to their various uses in the sentence. The particular form of the pronoun that is used is sometimes referred to as *case*. Thus, English pronouns have three *cases*: the *nominative* or *subjective* case is used when the pronoun acts as the subject of the clause or as a predicate nominative (*I am a citizen of the United States*, **He** *can speak fluent Arabic*, *It is* **we** *who shall prevail*). The *objective* (sometimes also called *oblique* or *accusative*) case is used when the pronoun acts as the object of a verb or pronoun (*The police officer stopped* **me** *for speeding*, *I gave* **him** *a gift for Christmas*, *They are talking about* **us**, *I left the books for* **them**). Finally, the *possessive* (sometimes also called *genitive*) case is used to indicate that the following noun or noun phrase belongs or pertains to the person indicated (i.e., to show possession: *That is* **my** *suitcase*, **Your** *tickets are ready*, *Nobody came to* **our** *house last night*). Some grammarians refer to these forms as **possessive adjectives** since they modify nouns and noun phrases. Included among the *possessive* pronoun forms are the *nominative possessives* (**mine, yours, ours,** and **theirs**), which are used when the pronoun stands alone and does not modify an overt noun or noun phrase (*That house is* **mine**; **Yours** *is fancier than* **his**; **Theirs** *are quite ugly, but* **ours** *are beautiful*).

When a personal pronoun is connected to another pronoun or noun with a coordinating conjunction, its case does not change (e.g., *John and* **I** *are going to Europe next week*, not **John and* **me** *are going to Europe next week*; *He gave the book to Chris and* **me**, not **He gave the book to Chris and* **I**). Also, when English combines a noun or pronoun with the first person pronoun in a noun phrase, the first person pronoun always comes last (e.g., *She gave the present to* **you and me**, not **She gave the present* to *me and you*; ***Mary and I*** *are working on a project together*, not *I and Mary are working on a project together).

Also, when we combine a pronoun and a noun, we use the case of the pronoun that would be appropriate if the pronoun were used alone (e.g., ***We three kings*** *of Orient are*, not ****Us three kings*** *of Orient are*; *That situation gave **us instructors** a bad name*, not **That situation gave **we instructors** a bad name*).

The following table summarizes the various forms of English **personal pronouns**.

TABLE 31. PERSONAL PRONOUNS

PERSON	SINGULAR			PLURAL		
CASE	*SUBJ.*	*OBJ.*	*POSS.*	*SUBJ.*	*OBJ.*	*POSS.*
FIRST	I	me	my/mine	we	us	our/ours
SECOND	you	you	your/yours	you	you	your/yours
THIRD	he she it	him her it	his/his her/hers its	they	them	their/theirs

Although as native English speakers we usually take such facts for granted, Standard English formally distinguishes two **numbers** (singular and plural) in the first and third persons, but only one **number** in the second person (the second person singular and plural pronoun is *you*). However, certain (non-standard) American English dialects do in fact make a distinction in the second person (for example, in Appalachian, Southern, and African-American English the second person plural pronoun is *y'all*, and in some Northeastern dialect areas the second person plural pronoun is **yous** or **you guys**). Furthermore, the third person *singular* pronouns distinguish three **genders** (masculine, feminine, and neuter), whereas the third person *plural* pronoun does not distinguish gender at all (**they** is the plural form of *he*, *she*, and *it*). While we as native speakers feel that this system is somehow normal or natural, it is important to understand there is nothing inherently natural about the English system of personal pronouns; in fact, cross-linguistically, the Modern English personal pronoun system is quite unusual and may present a number of difficulties for your students, who will likely speak a language with a substantially different pronominal system. For example, many languages make a **formality** or **politeness** distinction in the second person (e.g., Spanish *tú* and *Usted*), and most languages formally distinguish **number** for all persons, including the second person (e.g., French *tu* and *vous*, or early Modern English *thou* and *ye*). You must be sensitive to such linguistic differences when presenting this material to your students.

2.6.3 Reflexive pronouns

Reflexive pronouns (which have the same form as intensive pronouns) are used when an object in a clause refers to the same person or thing as the subject. Thus, whenever a **reflexive pronoun** is used in a clause, it *must* refer back to the subject (e.g., *I hurt **myself** lifting weights yesterday*, and *They bought the refrigerator for **themselves**, not for their daughter*). If a **reflexive pronoun** does not refer to the subject of the clause in which it appears, it should not be used (e.g., *If you have any questions, please contact Mr. Smith or me*, not **If you have any questions, please contact Mr. Smith or **myself***). Note that the reflexive pronoun **oneself** is used when the subject of a clause is the **indefinite pronoun** *one*.

X	I gave **me** a bath.
√	I gave **myself** a bath.
X	You are only hurting **you**.
√	You are only hurting **yourself**.
X	He (John) accidentally shot **him** (John).
√	He (John) accidentally shot **himself** (John).
√	He (John) accidentally shot **him** (Peter).
√	The dog bit **itself** in the foot.
√	The dog bit **it** (the cat) in the foot.
X	Please deliver the package directly to **myself**.
√	Please deliver the package directly to **me**.
√	One must have faith in **oneself**.
X	One must have faith in **himself**.

The same set of **reflexive pronouns** can also be used as **intensive pronouns**, which usually follow a noun or pronoun to add emphasis to it (e.g., *I **myself** don't eat red meat*, *They **themselves** did most of the work*). An **intensive pronoun** may precede the noun it modifies, although such a construction is somewhat unusual (***Myself**, I never drink and drive*).

Part 3: Presenting other Types of Words: Adjectives, Prepositions, and Adverbs

3.1 ADJECTIVES AND ADJECTIVE PHRASES

An adjective is a word that modifies or describes a noun or noun phrase (NP). English adjectives have at most three forms: the simple (base form)(e.g., *green*), the comparative form (e.g., *greener*), and the superlative form (e.g., *greenest*). Some adjectives (primarily those of three syllables or more) have only one form. Unlike many inflecting languages (such as Spanish, Russian, or Arabic), English adjectives do not change to reflect **number**, **gender**, or other grammatical categories.

3.2 PLACEMENT OF ADJECTIVES WITHIN THE CLAUSE

Although we often teach beginning students that the **adjective** usually precedes the noun or noun phrase that it modifies, this explanation is radically oversimplified to the point of being technically incorrect. In fact, the default position for English **adjectives** *without complements after the adjective* is directly before the modified noun or noun phrase. However, **adjectives** *with subsequent complements* **always** follow the noun or noun phrase being modified, and some **adjectives** without complements can come after the modified noun when the speaker wishes to add special emphasis. In addition, certain phrases (usually those borrowed from French, in which language the **adjective** frequently comes after the noun) contain postposed **adjectives**. Although such constructions are normally presented only to advanced students, you must understand these facts and be able to adequately exemplify them to students who inquire about them. The following table illustrates these rules.

√	That is a very **green** garden.	Adjective without complement
X	That is a garden very **green**.	Adjective without complement.
√	That Martian has **green** skin.	Adjective without complement.
X	She is a **green with envy** woman.	Adjective *with subsequent complement.*
√	She is a woman **green with envy**.	Adjective *with subsequent complement.*
√	That is a **very green** garden.	Adjective *with preceding modifier.*
√	I have a **full** tank of gas.	Adjective without complement
√	I have a tank **full of gas**.	Adjective *with subsequent complement.*
X	I have a **full of gas** tank.	Adjective *with subsequent complement.*
√	They sent the soldier to a **court-martial**.	Set phrase with *postposed adjective.*
√	John Ashcroft was an Attorney **General**.	Set phrase with *postposed adjective.*
√	John Ashcroft was a **general** attorney.	Adjective without complement.
?	They sent the soldier to a **martial court**.	Adjective without complement (see note).
√	Job, a man **tormented**, had great patience.	Adjective without complement *postposed for special emphasis.*
√	Job, a **tormented** man, had great patience.	Adjective without complement
√	I congratulated him on a job **well-done**.	Adjective with *implied* complement.
√	The gladiators engaged in a battle **royal**.	Set phrase with *postposed adjective.*
?	The gladiators engaged in a **royal** battle.	Adjective without complement

Note that in the above examples, *They sent the soldier to a **court-martial*** and *They sent the soldier to a **martial court*** have different meanings, as do *John Ashcroft was an **Attorney General*** and *John Ashcroft was a **general attorney***, and *The gladiators engaged in a **battle royal*** and *The gladiators engaged in a **royal battle***.

3.3 COMPARATIVE AND SUPERLATIVE FORMS OF ADJECTIVES

Sometimes we need to compare two nouns (or noun phrases); in order to do this, we use the **comparative** form of the adjective that modifies the noun. Most English adjectives form their **comparatives** in one of two ways: either the comparative suffix *–er* is added to the adjective, forming a single word (e.g., *greener* or *happier*), or the **comparative** adverb *more* precedes the adjective to create a comparative **adjective phrase** (e.g., *more expensive* or *more extravagant*). In a similar fashion, the **superlative** (that is, the most extreme degree of comparison) form of the adjective is formed either by adding the superlative suffix *–est* to the adjective, forming a single word (e.g., *greenest* or *happiest*), or by placing the **superlative** adverb *most* directly before the adjective to create a superlative **adjective phrase** (e.g., *most expensive* or *most extravagant*). Note, however, that the two methods of forming the **comparative** and **superlative** forms of adjectives are *never* mixed in Standard English (e.g., *That is the **longest** movie I've ever seen*, not **That is the **most longest** movie I've ever seen*).

Students frequently ask their instructors how to determine whether an adjective forms its **comparative** and **superlative** forms by adding suffixes or by placing *more* or *most* before the adjective. Contrary to what many students fear, it is not necessary to memorize which adjectives belong to which category. In fact, it is the phonological form of the adjective that dictates how its comparative and superlative forms are constructed. In general, adjectives of one or two *syllables* form their **comparative** and **superlative** forms by adding the suffixes *–er* and *–est*, while most adjectives of three syllables or more form their **comparative** and

superlative forms by preposing the adverbs *more* and *most*. However, a number of adjectives of two syllables (primarily those that end in consonants), and a handful of adjectives of a single syllable form their **comparative** and **superlative** forms using *more* and *most* when adding the **comparative** and **superlative** suffixes would lead to *phonotactic awkwardness* (that is, difficulty in pronouncing the word). In addition, **participles,** which are discussed in the following section, usually form their **comparative** and **superlative** forms using *more* and *most*, regardless of their number of syllables. Finally, the **negative comparative** adverbs *less* and *least* can be placed before *all* adjectives in order to indicate negative comparison (e.g., *The United States is **less populous** than China, Maria is the **least selfish** person I know*).

TABLE 32. COMPARATIVE AND SUPERLATIVE FORMS OF ADJECTIVES

Regular Form	Comparative	Superlative
young	younger	youngest
wild	wilder	wildest
true	truer	truest
lean	leaner	leanest
cold	colder	coldest
red	redder	reddest
near	nearer	nearest
crazy	crazier	craziest
happy	happier	happiest
ample	ampler	amplest
runny	runnier	runniest

TABLE 33. EXAMPLES OF ADJECTIVES OF ONE AND TWO SYLLABLES WHOSE COMPARATIVES AND SUPERLATIVES ARE FORMED WITH *MORE* AND *MOST* DUE TO PHONOTACTIC AWKWARDNESS

Regular Form	Comparative	Superlative
gold	more gold	most gold
live	more live	most live
blah	more blah	most blah
silver	more silver	most silver
learned	more learned	most learned
freezing	more freezing	most freezing
Latin	more Latin	most Latin
solemn	more solemn	most solemn
crowded	more crowded	most crowded
handsome	more handsome	most handsome
grateful	more grateful	most grateful

TABLE 34. EXAMPLES OF ADJECTIVES OF MORE THAN TWO SYLLABLES WHOSE COMPARATIVES AND SUPERLATIVES ARE FORMED WITH *MORE* AND *MOST*

Regular Form	Comparative	Superlative
wonderful	more wonderful	most wonderful
glorious	more glorious	most glorious
industrious	more industrious	most industrious
expensive	more expensive	most expensive
promising	more promising	most promising
destitute	more destitute	most destitute

3.3.1 Adjectives with irregular comparative and superlative forms

For historical linguistic reasons, a small handful of English adjectives form their **comparative** and **superlative** forms irregularly. Some of these adjectives use different stems when forming their **comparative** and **superlative** forms (a linguistic phenomenon technically known as *suppletion*), while others simply modify the adjectival root before adding the regular suffixes. The following table provides a list of these irregular adjectives. Unlike the **comparative** and **superlative** forms of most other adjectives, these forms must be memorized by students.

TABLE 35. IRREGULAR COMPARATIVE AND SUPERLATIVE FORMS OF ADJECTIVES

Regular Form	Comparative	Superlative
good	better	best
bad	worse	worst
far	farther or further	farthest or furthest
little	less	least
many	more	most
much	more	most

3.3.2 Using comparative and superlative forms of adjectives

When used in comparisons, the **comparative** forms of adjectives are usually followed by the word **than** (e.g., *John is **taller than** Bill, My car is **more efficient** than yours*). The comparative form of an adjective followed by **than** can also be combined with a noun (*You are a **better friend** than John, My sister has **more expensive clothes** than they do*). Note that in this type of construction, when a singular count noun is used after the adjective, the comparative form of the adjective follows the indefinite article *a/an* (e.g., *My grandmother is **an older woman** than my aunt*). We can also combine the **comparative** form of an adjective followed by **than** with longer phrases and clauses (e.g., *Food is **more expensive** in the big city **than** in the country, Learning to speak English becomes **easier** once you have studied it for a while **than** it is at first*). Also, when using the **comparative** form of an adjective, the second part of the comparison is sometimes omitted when it is considered obvious or understood (e.g., *Life doesn't get any **better** [than it is now], I would like to be **taller** [than I am now], I don't want to go any **farther** [than this]*). The **superlative** form of the adjective is usually preceded by **the** and is followed by the noun (or noun phrase) that it modifies (e.g., *Rome is **the nicest city** that I have ever visited, She is **the meanest woman** I know, You are **the most wonderful** mother in the world*).

3.4 PARTICIPLES AND GERUNDS

3.4.1 Present and past participles

A **participle** (the word *participle* is ultimately derived from the Latin for *partaker*) is a form of a verb that can function independently as an **adjective**. English has two participles—the **present participle**, which is always formed by adding the suffix *–ing* to the verbal stem, and the **past participle**, which is formed in a number of ways, although most (i.e., regular) verbs form their **past participles** simply by adding the suffix *–ed* to the verbal stem. The **past participle** of an irregular verb is usually formed by modifying the vowel of the verbal stem, adding an irregular suffix (typically *–en*), or both. In addition to acting as adjectives, **participles** also combine with **auxiliary verbs** to form compound verb tenses, as discussed earlier in this manual.

TABLE 36. PRESENT AND PAST PARTICIPLES

Verb	Present Participle	Past Participle
be	being	been
see	seeing	seen
go	going	gone
do	doing	done
eat	eating	eaten
write	writing	written
speak	speaking	spoken
think	thinking	thought
run	running	run
drink	drinking	drunk
jump	jumping	jumped
walk	walking	walked

Participles typically function in one of two ways: they either directly modify a noun or noun phrase (e.g., *That man is very **drunk**, The Grapes of Wrath is an extremely well-**written** book, Chess is very **boring***), or form **participle phrases** that can either precede or follow the noun or noun phrase they modify (e.g., ***Seeing** an opportunity to attack, Attila the Hun crossed the Volga; My mother, already **having** visited Europe, decided to vacation in Africa; **Soundly defeated**, the sprinter hung his head in shame*).

Like other adjectives, **participles** without (subsequent) complements are usually placed *before* the noun or noun phrases they modify, whereas those with complements that follow the **participle always** follow the modified noun or noun phrase.

However, when a participle has an unspoken but implied or understood complement, it may be placed *after* the noun or noun phrase it modifies.

√	Arnold Schwarzenegger was the **running** man.	Participle without complement
√	Arnold Schwarzenegger was the man **running** (from something or to somewhere).	Participle *with implied subsequent complement.*
√	He was the man **running from the law**.	Participle *with subsequent complement.*
X	He was the **running from the law** man.	Participle *with subsequent complement.*
√	*The Exorcist* was about a **possessed** child.	Participle without complement.
√	The soldier fought like a man **possessed** [by something].	Participle *with implied subsequent complement.*
X	*The Exorcist* was about a **possessed by a demon** child.	Participle *with subsequent complement.*
√	*The Exorcist* was about a child **possessed by a demon**.	Participle *with subsequent complement.*

3.4.2 Past participles and passive verbs

In addition to functioning as an adjective, the **past participle** is used to form **passive verbs**. **Passive verbs** are formed by the appropriately tensed form of the verb *to be* followed by the **past participle**, and serve to indicate that the grammatical *subject* of the verb is the *object* of the verbal action. In sentences such as *Video cassettes* **are being replaced** *by compact discs*, *Dinner* **will be served** *at 9 o'clock*, *The suspect* **was interrogated** *by the police*, *She* **has been seen** *by the doctor already*, and *I* **am** *completely* **shocked** *by your actions*, the grammatical subject is acted upon by either an explicit (e.g., *by the police*, *by the doctor*, and *by your actions*) or an implicit agent. **Passive verbs** are commonly used when the speaker either does not know or does not wish to indicate the agent acting upon the grammatical subject.

3.5 PREPOSITIONS AND PREPOSITIONAL PHRASES

A **preposition** is a word (or in a few cases, a phrase) usually placed before a noun or noun phrase (known as the *object of the preposition*) that indicates the relation of that noun or noun phrase to a verb, an adjective, or another noun or noun phrase. Common examples of prepositions include *at*, *by*, *with*, *from*, and *in regard to*. Although most of your students will be native speakers of languages that have **prepositions** that behave more or less like those found in English, you as an instructor should know that not all languages have prepositions—unlike verbs, nouns, and interjections, **prepositions** are not a universal lexical category. Some languages contain words that do the work of **prepositions** but are sometimes or always placed *after* their objects; these words are called **postpositions** (one well-known example of post-positioning is the Latin word *cum*, which means 'with,' and was always placed *after* personal pronoun objects, as in **mecum**, which means 'with me,' and is the ultimate ancestor of the Spanish word **conmigo**, which also means 'with me').

3.6 PREPOSITION STRANDING IN SPOKEN ENGLISH

In English, all **prepositions** must have objects. However, unlike the vast majority of other languages with **prepositions**, English permits **prepositions** to be *moved* away from their objects, so that the **preposition** no longer precedes the noun or noun phrase to which it was originally attached. This phenomenon, known as **preposition stranding**, is an extremely rare linguistic phenomenon that has been recorded in only a handful of languages, most of which are closely related to English (e.g., Danish and Dutch). **Preposition stranding**, which is an almost universal characteristic of modern spoken English, tends to be avoided in formal and semi-formal writing. It is also one of the most difficult aspects of English grammar for non-native speakers to master, and you should be prepared to find that some of your students may consider constructions involving stranded **prepositions** to be bizarre and illogical.

In **preposition stranding**, the **preposition** is moved from its original place *before* the noun or noun phrase object to clause-final position. In questions, this usually results in the **preposition** being moved from clause-initial to clause-final position. However, in other types of sentences this process is more complex, for in declarative sentences **preposition stranding** occurs when the original sentence contains a **prepositional phrase** with a *relative pronoun* as its **object**. In such sentences, the *relative pronoun object* is deleted and the **preposition** is moved, resulting in a defective **prepositional phrase** without an overt object. The following tables illustrate the process of **preposition stranding** in English.

TABLE 37. PREPOSITION STRANDING IN QUESTIONS

Question with **preposition unmoved.**	
About what	are you talking?
To who(m)	did you give the car?
From where	have you come?
Under what name	did you file it?
In what	will we believe?
Next to which chair	did you put it?
With who(m)	are you going?

Question with **preposition stranded.**		
What	are you talking	**about?**
Who(m)	did you give the car	**to?**
Where	have you come	**from?**
What name	did you file it	**under?**
What	will we believe	**in?**
Which chair	did you put it	**next to?**
Who(m)	are you going	**with?**

TABLE 38. PREPOSITION STRANDING IN DECLARATIVE SENTENCES

That is the school	**to which**	I went.		Sentence with intact prepositional phrase.
That is the school	**which**	I went	**to.**	Sentence with preposition stranded.
That is the school		I went	**to.**	Sentence with preposition stranded and relative pronoun object deleted.

In the example above, all three options are available to speakers and are considered grammatical. However, the sentence with the unmoved preposition (*That is the school **to which** I went*) is considered *extremely* formal and in most circumstances would be used only in writing. You should not encourage your students to use such constructions in everyday spoken English, but should make them aware that such forms are sometimes encountered in written English. Some other examples of **preposition stranding** in declarative sentences can be seen below.

Rio is the city	**in which**	I was born.		Sentence with intact prepositional phrase.
Rio is the city	**which**	I was born	**in.**	Sentence with preposition stranded.
Rio is the city		I was born	**in.**	Sentence with preposition stranded and relative pronoun object deleted.

In some situations, however, the relative pronoun object cannot be deleted. The rules regarding when the relative cannot be deleted are intricate and are in fact an object of linguistic debate; therefore, when presenting these structures to those students for whom it is appropriate, you should **exemplify** rather than **explain** this material.

?	I don't know	**about what**	you're talking.	
√	I don't know	**what**	you're talking	**about.**
X	I don't know		you're talking	**about.**

?	This is	**from where**	I come.	
√	This is	**where**	I come	**from.**
X	This is		I come	**from.**

3.7 PROBLEMS WITH THE MEANING OF CERTAIN PREPOSITIONS

As children learning English, we did not master the use and meaning of prepositions until relatively late in our language-learning phase. For some reason, learning and manipulating prepositions requires greater 'brainpower' than many other linguistic functions. Since the natural method of teaching a second language takes advantage of the same basic principles as learning one's native language, you should expect your students to experience some difficulties in mastering the *meaning* and *use* of certain prepositions.

Two of the most frequently encountered problems involve the differences in meaning and use between the prepositions *in* and *on*, and *to* and *toward*. Again, in presenting these prepositions to your students, **exemplify** rather than **explain** their differences.

TABLE 39. USING THE PREPOSITIONS *IN* AND *ON*

Some common meanings of the preposition *in*	Some common meanings of the preposition *on*
Within the limits, bounds, or area of. *He was hit **in** the face; I was born **in** France.*	Indicating position above and supported by or in contact with. *The money is **on** the table. We sat **on** a stool.*
From the outside to a point within; into. *He threw the letter **in** the trashcan. I fell **in** a ditch.*	Indicating contact with or extent over (a surface) regardless of position. *Hang the picture **on** the wall. You have a bump **on** your head.*
To or at a situation or condition. *Our nation is **in** debt. She is **in** love.*	Indicating figurative or abstract position. *He's **on** his third slice of pizza. Mary is a little **on** the young side.*
During the act or process of. *He fell **in** running for the bus.*	Indicating actual motion toward, against, or onto. *The asteroid fell **on** his barn.*
After the style or form of. *A poem **in** iambic pentameter.*	Indicating figurative or abstract motion toward, against, or onto. *My daughter is ten going **on** thirty. It's coming up **on** six o'clock.*
By means of. *He paid **in** cash. When in Europe, you must pay **in** euros.*	Indicating occurrence at a given time. *My birthday is **on** December 12. He comes every hour **on** the hour.*
With reference to. *I have faith **in** your judgment. I am six feet **in** height.*	Concerning or about. *I have a book **on** Julius Caesar. The teacher gave a talk **on** astronomy.*
Made with or through the medium of. *A statue **in** bronze. The book is written **in** Italian.*	Indicating the purpose, state, or process of something. *The building is **on** fire. Help is **on** the way.*

Notice that the differences in meaning and use between *in* and *on* are oftentimes subtle and that their usage is not predictable, as both prepositions frequently participate in idiomatic expressions (e.g., *The criminal was **in cahoots** with the Orion Crime Syndicate*, or *That man is high **on drugs***).

TABLE 40. USING OF THE PREPOSITIONS *TO* AND *TOWARD*

Some common meanings of the preposition ***to***	Some common meanings of the preposition ***toward***
In a direction toward, so as to reach. *We went **to** town to go shopping. She turned **to** me and said 'hello.'*	In the direction of. *We are driving **toward** the beach. The marathoner ran **toward** the finish line*
Reaching as far as. *The ocean was clear all the way **to** the bottom. I made it **to** the bank by closing time.*	In a position facing. *He had his back **toward** the wall. Turn **toward** the front and greet her.*
With the resultant condition of. *The doctor nursed me back **to** health.*	Somewhat before in time. *It started to snow **toward** evening.*
In front of or in contact with. *They stood face **to** face. They put their noses **to** the grindstone.*	With regard or in relation to. *You should always have an optimistic attitude **toward** life.*
Indicating appropriation or possession. *Where is the top **to** the jar?*	In furtherance or partial fulfillment of. *Please donate ten dollars **toward** cancer research.*
Concerning or regarding. *I am still waiting for a response **to** my question. **To** what end are you doing this?*	By way of achieving or with a view to. *Britain's diplomats have made many efforts **towards** peace with their enemies.*
For the purpose of. *We went out **to** dinner.*	
In a particular relationship with. *Interstate 95 runs parallel **to** Route 441.*	

Note that the preposition *toward* is sometimes rendered *towards*; the two prepositions are in free variation and there is no difference in meaning between the two variants. Also, **toward** sometimes has approximately the same meaning as **to** (e.g., *We are driving* **to** *the beach* and *We are driving* **toward** *the beach*).

3.8 ADVERBS

Adverbs (from the Latin *ad verbum*, or 'next to the verb') are words that modify verbs (or verb phrases), adjectives (or adjective phrases), or other adverbs. English adverbial morphology is relatively straightforward, as most **adverbs** are either underived words of a single morpheme (e.g., *only*, *just*, *very*) or are derived from adjectives through suffixation (e.g., *quickly*, *happily*, *unfortunately*, *simply*). Many English **adverbs** have been derived from adjectives, including some **participles**, by the addition of the adverbial suffix –*ly*. However, not all adjectives are susceptible to this process, as some otherwise possible adverbs, such as **fastly* for example, simply do not exist.

TABLE 41. ADVERBS DERIVED FROM ADJECTIVES

Adjective	+ ly	Derived Adverb
quick	ly	quickly
narrow	ly	narrowly
rough	ly	roughly
happy	ly	happily
fortunate	ly	fortunately
wry	ly	wryly
beautiful	ly	beautifully
calm	ly	calmly
whole	ly	wholly
wonderful	ly	wonderfully
true	ly	truly
just	ly	justly
jealous	ly	jealously
embarrassing	ly	embarrassingly
knowing	ly	knowingly
excited	ly	excitedly

Note that a smaller number of adjectives resist this process and do not permit suffixation. This list includes most adjectives that already end in –ly (e.g., *manly*, *gingerly*, etc.) and adverbs that have the same form as adjectives.

Adjective	+ ly	Derived Adverb
fast	ly	*fastly
red	ly	*redly
many	ly	*manily
early	ly	*earlily
few	ly	*fewly
little	ly	*littely
old	ly	*oldly
gingerly	ly	*gingerlily
manly	ly	*manlily

Finally, a small number of **adverbs** have the same form as **adjectives**.

TABLE 42. ADVERBS THAT HAVE THE SAME FORM AS ADJECTIVES

Adverb	Used as an adjective	Used as an adverb
hard	English is a **hard** language to learn.	If you study **hard**, you will learn English.
fast	I own a **fast** car.	I sometimes drive too **fast**.
early	The **early** bird gets the worm.	I have to wake up **early**.
straight	Use a ruler to draw a **straight** line.	For good posture one should sit up **straight**.
better	She is a **better** writer than I am.	She writes **better** than I do.

3.9 TYPES OF ADVERBS AND THE PLACEMENT OF ADVERBS WITHIN THE CLAUSE

Although English adverbial morphology is simple, adverbial syntax is extremely complex and will likely pose a significant challenge to your students. This is because much of the syntax related to **adverbs** is *lexically conditioned* (i.e., determined by the meaning—not the form—of the word). In general, **adverbs** are placed *next to* the constituent that they modify. However, when an **adverb** modifies an adjective or another adverb, it is usually placed directly *before* the modified word (e.g., *a **very** red shirt*, *an **extremely** disturbing phenomenon*, *the **just** completed project*). In some cases, placement of the **adverb** depends on whether it modifies a verb (e.g., *I would have **never** done that*: **never** modifies the verb *done*) or an entire verb phrase (e.g., *I **never** would have done that*: **never** modifies the verb phrase *would have done that*).

3.9.1 Adverbs of manner, frequency, degree, place, and time

Adverbs of manner, one of the largest group of **adverbs**, answer the question *how?* and are generally placed *after* the verb phrases that they modify (i.e., *after* verbs without direct objects or *after* the direct object if the verb has one). This group of **adverbs** includes most **adverbs** derived from adjectives.

TABLE 43. ADVERBS OF MANNER

The runner	ran	**quickly, slowly, rapidly.**
The President	spoke	**loudly, softly, angrily, aggressively.**
She	did her job	**well.**
Susan	wrote the letter	**neatly.**
The dancer	moved	**gracefully,** like a swan.
Argentina	performed	**admirably, poorly** in the World Cup.
The Red Cross	delivered the food	**hastily** but **efficiently** to the victims.
The professor	graded the tests	**strictly** as well as **fairly.**

Adverbs of frequency describe *when* an action takes place. This group of **adverbs** includes *only, always, often, sometimes, still, never* (and *ever*), *hardly, frequently, rarely, seldom,* and *usually,* among others. These adverbs are typically placed directly *before* the main verb, but *after* the verb *to be* when *to be* is not an auxiliary verb.

TABLE 44. ADVERBS OF FREQUENCY

Mr. Smith	has	**never**	gone	to Hollywood.
You	would have	**only**	seen	her at work.
My friends	**are**	**usually**		with me.
I		**always**	eat	lunch at home.
We	could not have	**ever**	done	it without you.
My dog	**is**	**rarely**		that friendly.
John	had	**hardly**	woken up	when the phone rang.
My son	will	**seldom**	come	home on holidays.

Adverbs of degree describe the intensity or degree of an action. These **adverbs** include *almost, nearly, quite, just, too, also, enough, hardly, scarcely,* and *completely*. These **adverbs** are usually placed *before* the adjective or adverb being modified (e.g., *It is **too** cold in this room, We have **almost** enough space to seat twenty guests*) and, like **adverbs of time and manner**, directly *before* the main verb.

TABLE 45. ADVERBS OF DEGREE

She	doesn't	**quite**	understand	how this happened.
They	have	**completely**	exhausted	their savings.
John	should have	**just**	arrived	at the airport.
I	am	**too**	tired	to go out tonight.
We	were	**just**	leaving	when you arrived.
We	have had	**quite**	enough	of your complaining.
John	had	**hardly**	woken up	when the phone rang.
My son	will	**seldom**	come	home on holidays.
They	are	**also**	studying	Chinese.

Adverbs of place, such as *here, there, nowhere, anywhere, out, up, down, back, around, toward/towards* and *away*, answer the question *where?* and are usually placed *after* the direct object or the verb, although *here* and *there* can sometimes be placed *before* the verb phrase.

TABLE 46. ADVERBS OF PLACE

She	looked	**away, up, down, around, over.**
They	are going	**there, back, nowhere, anywhere.**
My friend	came	**out** of the house and ran **towards** me.
Nobody	is	**there, here, around, away.**
Here	they are.	
There	it goes.	

Adverbs of time indicate *when* the action takes place. This group of **adverbs** includes *soon, later, now, then, again, afterwards, finally, today, yesterday, tomorrow,* and *permanently*, among others. Generally, **adverbs of time** are placed at the *beginning* or *end* of a clause (and a few can be placed at either location).

TABLE 47. ADVERBS OF TIME

	I'm very busy	today.
	I went to the gym	again.
Afterwards	they ate lunch.	
	We will be back	tomorrow.
Yesterday	they went out to dinner.	
	They went out to dinner	yesterday.
Now	it's really pouring.	
	Dinner will be ready	soon.
Today	it will be sunny and dry.	
	It will be sunny and dry	today.
Then	I came home and went to bed.	

3.9.2 Clause-final adverbs (*too, as well, either*, etc.)

Finally, a small number of **adverbs** are usually placed at the end of clause. This group includes *too, yet, as well,* and *either*.

TABLE 48. CLAUSE-FINAL ADVERBS

I want to go to New York,	**too.**
My mother speaks French	**as well.**
Our plane hasn't arrived	**yet.**
Did you make the reservation	**yet?**
Are you coming	**as well?**
Will she be there	**too?**
I'm not coming,	**either.**

3.10 COMPARATIVE AND SUPERLATIVE FORMS OF ADVERBS

With the exception of a few irregular **adverbs** (*well*, *badly*, and *soon*, for instance), the **comparative** and **superlative** of **adverbs** are formed in the same manner as are formed the comparative and superlative forms of adjectives of more than two syllables (that is, by the addition of *more* and *most* before the **adverb** in question). However, unlike most adjectives, many **adverbs** cannot logically exist in a comparative state. For example, what meaning would *more as well* or *most quite* have? Thus, as a rule, only **adverbs of manner** and some **adverbs of frequency** exist in **comparative** and **superlative** form. A few **adverbs** have irregular **comparative** and **superlative** forms; these **adverbs** are listed below and are usually **adverbs** that have the same form as adjectives (whence their comparative and superlative forms are derived).

TABLE 49. COMPARATIVE AND SUPERLATIVE FORMS OF ADVERBS

Adverb	Comparative form	Superlative form
soon	sooner	soonest
late	later	latest
well	better	best
badly	worse	worst
far	farther or further	farthest or furthest
early	earlier	earliest
fast	faster	fastest
quickly	more quickly	most quickly
frequently	more frequently	most frequently
seldom	more seldom	most seldom
often	more often	most often
lovingly	more lovingly	most lovingly
today	**no comparative form**	**no superlative form**
again	**no comparative form**	**no superlative form**
sometimes	**no comparative form**	**no superlative form**

3.11 PROBLEMS WITH THE MEANING OF CERTAIN ADVERBS AND ADJECTIVES

Although students generally do not find English **adverbs** difficult to master, they sometimes confuse and incorrectly use a few **adverbs** with similar meanings. The adverbs *very, so, too,* and *a lot* all imply a *high or excessive degree* or a *large number or quantity*, as does the adjective *too much*, which is sometimes confused with these **adverbs**. However, each of these **adverbs** has its own subtleties and shades of meaning and differs from the others in important ways. Remember, the best way to guide your students toward a solid understanding of how to use these **adverbs** correctly is exemplification and practice.

TABLE 50. COMMONLY CONFUSED ADVERBS

Adverb	Definition(s)	Examples of use
very	In a high degree; extremely. Truly; absolutely.	It is **very** hot in Mexico. A **very** great number of people live in New York. This is the **very** same book I saw in the library.
so	To the amount or degree expressed or understood. To a great extent or such an evident degree.	She was **so** tired that she fell asleep. Some truths are **so** obvious that they need no explanation.
too	More than enough; excessively. Very, immensely, or extremely (less common).	My mistake was all **too** apparent. **Too** many accidents are taking place on the highways nowadays. He's only **too** willing to help.
a lot	To a very great degree or extent. Synonym: **very much**.	We enjoyed ourselves **a lot**. This would help us **a lot**. It rained **a lot** on our trip to Hawaii.
too much (adjective)	Being excessive or unreasonable.	That car cost entirely **too much**. That outfit is a bit **too much**. It rained **too much** on our trip to Hawaii.

3.12 PROBLEMS WITH THE MEANING OF CERTAIN ADVERBS AND ADJECTIVES: NO AND NOT

In many languages, a single word serves to express refusal or denial on the one hand, and to negate the verb on the other. However, English is not such a language. The word *no* is both an adjective and an adverb in English, and is used as the negative answer to a question (as an adverb) and to modify a noun or noun phrase (as an adjective) to indicate *not any*, *not one*, or *not at all*. The word *not* is always an **adverb**, and is used to express negation, denial, refusal, or prohibition when modifying a verb, and means *in no way* or *to no degree* when modifying an adjective or adverb. The most important difference between *no* and *not* is that *no* is used to answer questions, and *not* is used to negate verbs.

As an adjective, *no* is always placed directly before the noun or noun phrase that it modifies.

TABLE 51. USING *NO* AND *NOT*

The thief showed his victims	**no**	mercy.
I have	**no**	money left.
The detective left	**no**	stone unturned in his investigation.
	No	man is an island unto himself.

As an adverb, *no* is used to express denial or answer a question.

No,	I'm not going.
No,	you're wrong.
No,	we didn't.

The adverb *no* can also modify an adjective, when it is often used with the comparative.

They are	**no**	better	than you.
IBM is	**no**	longer	making fax machines.
Unfortunately, we have	**no**	more	cookies to sell.

The adverb *not* is used to negate the verb. When the main verb is *to be*, *not* follows the verb. However, for all other verbs, *not* must precede the main verb and be preceded itself by an auxiliary verb. As discussed earlier, *not* frequently contracts with the auxiliary verb preceding it.

They are	**not**	better	than you.
IBM is	**not**	making	fax machines any more.
Unfortunately, we have	**not**	made	enough cookies to sell.
We should	**not**	leave	before saying goodbye.
The dinosaurs did	**not**	survive	the famous meteor crash in Mexico.

The adverb *not* may also modify adjectives and other adverbs, or be placed before a noun or noun phrase for emphasis.

	Not	all	elephants are friendly.
	Not	everyone	likes chocolate cake.
I have seen	**not**	a single	person outside tonight.
She bought	**not**	only	a new car but also a new truck.
When I was there, I saw	**not**	even	one famous person.
I speak	**not**	one,	but three languages.

Part 4: Presenting English Syntax

4.1 AN OVERVIEW OF ENGLISH SYNTAX

Syntax refers to the principles whereby words or other elements of sentence structure are combined to form grammatical sentences. Stated more simply, **syntax** is all about correct word order. As you have already read, English **syntax** is relatively complicated as compared to its *morphology* (i.e., the structure and form of words, including inflection, derivation, and the formation of compounds). This is particularly true for the formation of questions, considered by many to be one of the most vexing aspects of English grammar.

Although the *default* word order for English declarative sentences is subject-verb-object (SVO), a number of seeming exceptions exist in which the verb *precedes* the subject. However, at a fundamental level such constructions are not really exceptions at all but are rather manifestations of a deeper level of syntactic organization that requires the verb to be the **second** fundamental constituent in the clause. In presenting English syntax to your students, you will encounter two primary areas of concern for your students: first, students must master the various syntactic constructions used in the formation of interrogative sentences (i.e., questions); and second, they must recognize the circumstances in which the *default* SVO word order is 'violated' and the **V2 rule or principle** (i.e., the rule or principle requiring the verb to be the second fundamental constituent in the clause) invoked.

4.2 QUESTION FORMATION: SUBJECT-VERB INVERSION

4.2.1 Forming questions with auxiliary verbs

The formation of questions in English generally requires two syntactic elements: the use of an *auxiliary* verb and inversion of the **subject** and **verb** (i.e., the **verb** must *precede* the **subject**). The only apparent exception to this rule involves questions with the verb *to be*, which does not require an additional *auxiliary verb* since it is itself an *auxiliary* verb, notwithstanding the fact that it is the main verb in the clause. If a question does not otherwise require the use of a specific *auxiliary verb*, then the default *auxiliary verb to do* is used.

For yes/no questions that use the *auxiliary verbs* **to have** or **to be** (with the present participle), or *modal auxiliary verbs*, simply **invert** the **subject** and **verb**.

TABLE 52. FORMING *YES/NO* QUESTIONS WITH AUXILIARY VERBS

Declarative Sentence	John	has	been	to Munich.
Question	Has	John	been	to Munich?
Declarative Sentence	He	is	going	to the conference.
Question	Is	he	going	to the conference?
Declarative Sentence	Mona	can	speak	French
Question	can	Mona	speak	French

For *yes/no* questions that do not otherwise require the use an *auxiliary verb* (that is, the answer to the question does not use an *auxiliary verb*), use the default *auxiliary verb* **to do**.

Declarative Sentence	They	like		chocolate cake.
Question	Do	they	like	chocolate cake?

Declarative Sentence	They	went		to New York.
Question	Did	they	go	to New York?

Declarative Sentence	You	saw		the Statue of Liberty.
Question	Did	you	see	the Statue of Liberty?

Finally, for *yes/no* questions that use the verb **to be** as the main verb, simply invert the **subject** and **verb**.

TABLE 53. FORMING *YES/NO* QUESTIONS WITH THE VERB *TO BE*

Declarative Sentence	They	are		from Canada.
Question	Are	they		from Canada?

Declarative Sentence	I	am		American.
Question	Am	I		American?

4.2.2 Forming questions with negated auxiliary verbs

When the speaker anticipates that the answer to a yes/no question is in the affirmative, the *auxiliary verb* used in the formation of the question is negated by the adverb *not*. This process is usually manifested with a contracted form of the adverb *not* attached to the *auxiliary verb*. However, the adverb *not* may also be placed *after* the **subject** for emphatic or formal effect; such constructions are fairly rare.

TABLE 54. FORMING QUESTIONS WITH NEGATED AUXILIARY VERBS

Declarative Sentence	They	like		chocolate cake.
Question	Don't	they	like	chocolate cake?
Emphatic question	Do	they	**not** like	chocolate cake?
Declarative Sentence	John	has	been	to Munich.
Question	Hasn't	John	been	to Munich?
Emphatic question	Has	John	**not** been	to Munich?
Declarative Sentence	They	are		from Canada.
Question	Aren't	they		from Canada?
Emphatic question	Are	they	**not**	from Canada?

Because there is no contraction for *am not* in Standard English, we sometimes use *aren't* as the negated verb for this type of yes/no question when the subject is *I*. Although this form is commonly used in spoken English, it should be avoided in writing in favor of the emphatic form.

Declarative Sentence	I	am		American.
Question	**Aren't**	I		American?
Emphatic question	Am	I	**not**	American?

4.3 FORMING QUESTIONS WITH WH-WORDS

Obviously, not all questions can be answered with *yes* or *no*. Open-ended questions require the use of a **wh-word** or (usually prepositional) phrase including a **wh-word**. **Wh-words** are words used to ask a questions, and include *who, whose, what, which, when, where, why,* and *how*. In general, such questions always *begin* with the **wh-word**, even if the **wh-word** is not the **subject** of the sentence (**wh-words** can serve as the **subject** or **object** of a clause, or they can be **adjectives** or **adverbs**). Questions formed with **wh-words** still require the use of an *auxiliary verb*, unless the main verb is *to be*, and require **subject**-**verb** inversion unless the **wh-word** is acting as the **subject** of the clause.

TABLE 55. FORMING QUESTIONS WITH WH-WORDS

Question	What	will	they	do for Thanksgiving?
Answer	They	will		go to grandma's house.

Question	When	are	they	going on vacation?
Answer	They	are		going on vacation next week.

Question	Which	would	they	prefer?
Answer	They	would		prefer that one.

Question	How	can	we	get there?
Answer	We	can		take a train.

Question	**Whose car**	should	we	use to go to the ballgame?
Answer	We	should		use my car.

Like all questions, if the answer does not require the use of an *auxiliary verb*, then the question must use the default *auxiliary verb* **to do**.

Question	**Where**	did	you	put the tray?
Answer	I	put		it under the coffee table.

Question	**Why**	do	we	study English?
Answer	We	study		so that we may learn.

Question	**When**	did	you	arrive?
Answer	I	arrived		last night.

Question	**How**	did	you	do that?
Answer	I	did		it with a knife.

If the **wh-word** acts as or modifies the **subject** of the clause, no **inversion** is necessary, as **inverting** the **subject** and the **verb** would move the **wh-word** out of its required clause-initial position.

Question	**Who**	will	(empty)	go with them?
Answer	Janice	will		go with them.

Question	**How many** people	were	(empty)	on the train?
Answer	Thirty people	were		on the train.

In some cases, the **wh-word** will be contained within a **prepositional phrase**. This type of question follows all the normal rules for question formation: the **prepositional phrase** containing the **wh-word** acts as a unit and is the first constituent in the sentence, and **subject-verb** inversion takes place.

Question	Under **what** letter	did	you	file that case?
Answer	I	filed		it under 'W.'

Question	On **whose** authority	has	he	relied?
Answer	He	has relied		on my authority.

Question	Next to **which** box	can	they	put the briefcase?
Answer	They	can		put it next to the red one.

However, as you may recall from the earlier section on **prepositional phrases**, speakers often **strand the preposition** at the end of the sentence in everyday spoken English. In questions with **wh-words** contained within a **prepositional phrase**, the **object of the preposition** (which contains the **wh-word**) begins the sentence, **subject-verb inversion** takes place, and the **preposition** is moved and stranded to the end of the sentence.

PRESENTING ENGLISH GRAMMAR

Question	**What** letter	did	you	file that case	**under?**
Answer	I	filed		that case	under 'W.'

Question	**Whose** authority	has	he	relied	**on?**
Answer	He	has		relied	on my authority.

Question	**Which** box	can	they	put the case	**next to?**
Answer	They	can		put the case	next to that box.

4.4 USING QUESTION TAGS

In addition to asking yes/no questions through **subject-verb inversion**, English speakers sometimes use an alternative method of question formation when they presume to know the answer to a question. By adding short interrogative clauses called **question tags** to the end of a declarative sentence, speakers seek to verify information that they already believe to be true (or untrue).

Although speakers of many languages use **question tags** for similar functions, the syntactic rules associated with the use of **question tags** vary greatly from language to language; as a result, your students may find the concept of **question tags** familiar, but may nevertheless have difficulty using them correctly. The following table illustrates the use of **question tags** in English.

TABLE 56. EXAMPLES OF QUESTION TAGS

You **speak** German,	**don't** you?
Everyone **came** to dinner,	**didn't** they?
You **have** laryngitis,	**don't** you?
John **is** from Portland,	**isn't** he?
They**'re** coming soon,	**aren't** they?
England **will** win the World Cup,	**won't** it?
We **can** go on vacation next month,	**can't** we?
I **should** help her,	**shouldn't** I?
They **would** have already done it,	**wouldn't** they?
It**'s** rained twice this week,	**hasn't** it?
Your friends **have** eaten lunch already,	**haven't** they?

As you can see from the table above, questions of this type are formed by adding a short interrogative clause, known as a **question tag**, to the declarative sentence whose validity the speaker wishes to confirm. For students, the most difficult part of using **question tags** involves the choice of **auxiliary verb** to be used in the **question tag**. However, in using **question tags**, English speakers follow a few simple rules. First, the **subject** and **verb** of the interrogative clause are inverted. Second, if an **auxiliary verb** is used in the declarative clause, then the same **auxiliary verb** is the verb used in the **question tag**. If *no auxiliary verb* is used in the declarative clause, then the default **auxiliary verb *to do*** is used in the appropriate tense (i.e., either simple present or simple past). Finally, if the verb used in the declarative clause is in the affirmative, then the verb used in the **question tag** will be in the negative. Conversely, if the verb used in the declarative clause is in the negative, then the verb used in the **question tag** will be in the affirmative. When the speaker believes that the answer to the question is *yes*, the verb used in the declarative clause is in the affirmative. On the other hand, if the speaker believes that the answer to the question is *no*, then the verb used in the declarative sentence is in the negative.

TABLE 57. USING QUESTION TAGS

Declarative Clause	Question tag	The speaker thinks...
You **speak** German,	**don't** you?	Answer is **yes.**
You **don't speak** German,	**do** you?	Answer is **no.**
You **have** laryngitis,*	**don't** you?	Answer is **yes.**
You **don't have** laryngitis,*	**do** you?	Answer is **no.**
They**'re** coming soon,	**aren't** they?	Answer is **yes.**
They**'re not** coming soon,	**are** they?	Answer is **no.**
We **can** go on vacation next month,	**can't** we?	Answer is **yes.**
We **can't** go on vacation next month,	**can** we?	Answer is **no.**
They **would** have already done it,	**wouldn't** they?	Answer is **yes.**
They **wouldn't** have already done it,	**would** they?	Answer is **no.**
Your friends **have** eaten lunch,*	**haven't** they?	Answer is **yes.**
Your friends **haven't** eaten lunch,*	**have** they?	Answer is **no.**

*__Remember__: when the verb *to have* is used as the **main verb**, it does not contract with *not* and requires the use of the auxiliary verb *to do* when used in questions. When the verb *to have* is used as an auxiliary verb, it can contract and can be used as the (only) verb in questions and **question tags**. In addition, **question tags** are generally not formed with *may* and *ought to*, and **question tags** formed with *shall*, *must*, and *might* are becoming archaic and sound affected to many speakers.

4.5 INDIRECT (REPORTED) QUESTIONS

Indirect (also known as **reported** or **embedded**) **questions** are simply **relative clauses** that begin with a **wh-word** and therefore have the superficial appearance of questions (e.g., *I know **where you live**; We don't know **how they got there***). However, **indirect questions** are not questions and, as a result, do not require the use of an **auxiliary verb** or permit **subject-verb** inversion, even when they function as clauses subordinate to an actual question (e.g., *Do you know **where he lives?***). For many of your students, the use of **indirect questions** will not be a problem. However, in some languages related to English (such as Spanish), **indirect questions** require **subject-verb inversion**. Thus, for those students whose native languages require **subject-verb inversion** in **indirect questions**, you may need to use many clear examples or even make special mention of the fact that English neither permits nor requires **subject-verb inversion** in **indirect questions**.

√	I know **who he is.**
X	I know **who is he.**
√	They saw **what I did.**
X	They saw **what did I.**
X	They saw **what did I do.**
√	**Who(m) she saw** is a mystery.
X	**Who(m) saw she** is a mystery.
X	**Who(m) did she see** is a mystery.
√	You heard **how well I shot the ball.**
X	You heard **how well shot I the ball.**
X	You heard **how well did I shoot the ball.**
√	Do you know **when they're coming?**
X	Do you know **when are they coming?**
√	Will you tell us **why you did it?**
X	Will you tell us **why did you it?**
X	Will you tell us **why did you do it?**

4.6 REGULAR WORD ORDER (SVO) IN DECLARATIVE SENTENCES

In general and as a rule, the regular, default word order of a declarative sentence (and of declarative clauses in general) in English is **subject-verb-object** (or **SVO**). Although there are a number of different constructions in which the verb precedes the subject, such structures are the exception to English syntax, not the rule. However, the object almost **never** precedes the subject in Modern English (a scant few exceptions to this almost inviolable rule can be found in the works of a handful of poets). In fact, languages that regularly permit the object to precede the subject are rare cross-linguistically; such languages are so uncommon that until very recently, linguists had believed that no human languages that had **OSV** or **VOS** as their default word order existed.

Most of your students will be native speakers of languages that prefer syntactic constructions in which the **subject** precedes the **verb**. Consequently, successfully mastering English's default **SVO** word order will not be a problem for the vast majority of your students. Unfortunately (for your students), most languages do not permit the types of constructions used in English and explained below in which the **verb** precedes the **subject** (excepting questions, of course). As a result, you may need to spend a significant amount of class time focusing on such constructions.

4.7 IMPERSONAL CLAUSES

Although all English sentences (with the exception of imperative clauses) must have an overt **subject**, many kinds of sentences have no natural **subject**; clauses that lack a natural **subject** are known as **impersonal clauses**. In such constructions, either *it* or *there* occupies the **subject position**. Note that for **impersonal** clauses that begin with *there*, the **subject** will always follow the **verb** (because technically, *there* is an adverb, not a pronoun).

4.7.1 Impersonal *it*

English speakers use the impersonal *it* when talking about the weather, identifying things, talking about time or distance, or simply noting that a thing or situation has a certain characteristic or feature. Although most impersonal clauses use a form of the verb **to be**, other stative verbs may be used (e.g., *to happen* or *to occur*, or verbs related to the weather, such as *to rain* or *to snow*). In these types of clauses, the pronoun *it* may not have an antecedent (i.e., a noun or noun phrase to which it refers), or may have only a very abstract antecedent (such as *the weather* or *the time*), and often exists simply to fill the obligatory **subject** slot in the clause. Impersonal clauses that begin with *it* often pose a problem for our students because in many languages, analogous constructions do not require the presence of an overt **subject**. In fact, a great many languages do not have a word that corresponds to the English impersonal *it*.

TABLE 58. USING THE IMPERSONAL *IT*

Talking about weather	It's raining. It's too hot to go outside. It was cold last night. It snowed yesterday. It will be sunny all day.
Identifying something	It's a bird. Who was **it**? It was John. What is **it**? It's an alligator.
Talking about time and the date	It's three o'clock. What time is **it**? What year is **it**? It's 2005. What day is **it**? It's Monday. It's Christmas today!
Talking about distance	How far is **it** to New York? It's 1200 miles. Is **it** close to the park? It's right next door. It's a long way to San Jose.
Noting a characteristic or feature	It's a shame that she left. It was a mistake. It's never easy to say goodbye. It's a pity.
Using certain stative verbs	It just so happens that today is my birthday. It occurred to me that he's right.
Passive constructions	It was thought that he was murdered. It is rumored that the queen is getting married. Was **it** already known in 1492 that the world was round?

4.7.2 Impersonal *there*

English speakers use the impersonal **there** to express that something exists, or that something exists in a particular place or state. In most instances, the verb used in such constructions is **to be**, although as for impersonal clauses that begin with **it**, other stative verbs may be used. Remember that the **subject** of an impersonal **there** clause follows the verb and that *there* is not the **subject** of the clause; thus, the verb must agree in **number** with the noun or noun phrase **subject** that follows it.

Make sure that your students do not confuse impersonal **there** clauses with clauses that begin with **they are.** Because sentences such as *There are nice people over there* and *They are nice people over there* sound similar, students may confuse these structures. Explain to your students that such sentences have different meanings, as the first emphasizes the existence of *nice people* at a specific place (*over there*), whereas the second points to a specific group of *nice people* (specifically, *they*) that happen to be *over there*. Grammatically, the **subject** of the first sentence is *nice people*, while the **subject** of the second sentence is *they*.

TABLE 59. USING THE IMPERSONAL *THERE*

Singular	Plural
There is a fly on my desk.	**There** are three flies on my desk.
There's a man waiting in your office.	**There** are two men waiting in your office.
There isn't enough time.	**There** aren't enough minutes in the day.
Is **there** anyone here?	Are **there** any people here?
Was **there** a party last night?	Were **there** any parties last night?
There is nobody here.	**There** were four people there.
There was a certain sound to his voice.	**There** were certain sounds to his voice.
Will **there** be any cake left?	Will **there** be any cakes left?
There goes the neighborhood.	**There** go the neighborhoods.
There seems to be something wrong.	**There** seem to be a few problems.
There appears to be enough money.	**There** appear to be some coins missing.
There happens to be a problem.	**There** happen to be a few problems.

4.8 SUBJECT-VERB INVERSION IN DECLARATIVE SENTENCES

Although the normal, default word order of an English declarative sentence is **SVO**, there are a few constructions that require the **verb** to precede the **subject**. Technically, such constructions require that the **verb** be the second constituent in the clause, bumping the **subject** to third position. However, in presenting these structures to your students, you should simply point out that in a few special cases, the **verb** comes before the **subject**.

4.8.1 Subject-verb inversion with initial negative adverbs and prepositional phrases

The first such special case involves sentences that begin with a **negative adverb** (or adverb phrase) or **negative prepositional phrase**. When the speaker begins a sentence with **negative adverbs** such as *hardly, rarely, never, scarcely,* or *no sooner* (among others), or with a **negative prepositional phrase** such as *under no circumstances, in no way,* or *by no means* (among others), the **verb** must immediately follow, and the **subject** must come after the verb. In such constructions, as in questions and most other constructions in which the verb precedes the subject, **an auxiliary verb** must be used. Remember that *to be* counts as an **auxiliary verb** even when used alone, and that if an **auxiliary verb** is not otherwise needed, then the default **auxiliary verb** *to do* must be used. Keep in mind that English speakers begin sentences with **negative adverbs** or **negative prepositional phrases** to place special emphasis on the adverb or prepositional phrase in question, and that the adverb or prepositional phrase is not required to come first in the sentence; speakers always have the option of beginning the sentence normally with a **subject** and **verb**, placing the **negative adverb** or **negative prepositional phrase** elsewhere in the sentence. Examples of these constructions are illustrated below.

√	**Never**	have	I seen such a beautiful sight.
X	**Never**		I have seen such a beautiful sight.
√			I have **never** seen such a beautiful sight.
√	**Rarely**	does	she eat so much.
X	**Rarely**		she eats so much.
√			She **rarely** eats so much.
√	**Hardly ever**	do	I speak Russian.
X	**Hardly ever**		I speak Russian.
√			I **hardly ever** speak Russian.
√	**Not very often**	will	you hear of something like that.
X	**Not very often**		you will hear of something like that.
√			You **won't very often** hear of something like that.
√	**In no way**	must	this reflect poorly on my record.
X	**In no way**		this must reflect poorly on my record.
√			This must **in no way** reflect poorly on my record.
√	**By no means**	should	you quit the race.
X	**By no means**		you should quit the race.
√			You should **by no means** quit the race.
√	**At no time**	shall	you leave the confines of this prison.
X	**At no time**		you shall leave the confines of this prison.
√			You shall **at no time** leave this prison.

4.8.2 Subject-verb inversion with conditional clauses beginning with *were* and *had*

The second case in which the **verb** precedes the **subject** in declarative sentences involves **conditional clauses** in which the *if* is omitted. An alternative method of forming the **second conditional** when the verb in the **condition clause** is *to be* is to omit the *if* and then invert the **subject** and **verb**. Similarly, the **third conditional** may alternatively be formed by omitting the *if* and inverting the **subject** and **verb** (i.e., *had*). This process occurs only when the **conditional clause** precedes the **result clause**. This process is exemplified below.

TABLE 60. ALTERNATE METHOD OF FORMING THE SECOND CONDITIONAL WITH SUBJECT-VERB INVERSION

Method	Condition clause	Result clause
Normal (SVO)	If I were you, If he were here, If Maria were younger, If they were to do that, If we were smarter,	I wouldn't do that. he would say yes. she would want to go. they might win. we would stop.
Subject-verb inversion	Were I you, Were he here, Were Maria younger, Were they to do that, Were we smarter,	I wouldn't do that. he would say yes. she would want to go. they might win. we would stop.

TABLE 61. ALTERNATE METHOD OF FORMING THE THIRD CONDITIONAL WITH SUBJECT-VERB INVERSION

Method	Condition clause	Result clause
Normal (SVO)	If I had known, If he had been there, If Maria had been younger, If they had done that, If we had been smarter,	I wouldn't have done that. he would have said yes. she would have gone. they might have won. we would have stopped.
Subject-verb inversion	Had I known, Had he been there, Had Maria been younger, Had they done that, Had we been smarter,	I wouldn't have done that. he would have said yes. she would have gone. they might have won. we would have stopped.

4.8.3 Subject-verb inversion with initial adverbs and stative verbs

The next case in which the **verb** precedes the **subject** in a declarative clause is a rather uncommon one. When the sentence begins with an adverb (or adverb phrase) or prepositional phrase of location or condition, and the main **verb** is a **stative verb**, then the **verb** must precede the **subject**. Such constructions do not involve objects, since **stative verbs** are by their nature intransitive and thus cannot take objects. However, like other declarative constructions in which the **verb** precedes the **subject**, the **verb** is only required to precede the **subject** if some syntactic constituent **other than the subject** begins the sentence. Thus, the speaker is always free to employ the normal **SV(O)** word order and place the adverb or prepositional phrase in its normal position. Examples of this phenomenon are illustrated below.

√	**Here**	lies	the body of poor old Jesse James.
?	**Here**		the body of poor old Jesse James lies.
√			The body of poor old Jesse James lies **here**.
√	**Over the horizon**	sits	the Rock of Gibraltar.
X	**Over the horizon**		the Rock of Gibraltar sits.
√			The Rock of Gibraltar sits **over the horizon**.
√	**In this house**	lives	the ghost of Mr. Spencer.
?	**In this house**		the ghost of Mr. Spencer lives.
√			The ghost of Mr. Spencer lives **in this house**.
√	**Nearby**	hangs	the Mona Lisa.
X	**Nearby**		the Mona Lisa hangs.
√			The Mona Lisa hangs **nearby**.
√	**Under that rock**	rest	the remains of a Stoneage farmer.
X	**Under that rock**		the remains of a Stoneage farmer rest.
√			The remains of a farmer rest **under that rock**.
√	**Above her head**	dangles	a shiny halo.
?	**Above her head**		a shiny halo dangles.
√			A shiny halo dangles **above her head**.

4.8.4 Subject-verb inversion with *so* and *neither*

The final case in which the **verb** precedes the **subject** in declarative sentences involves fixed expressions that follow the formula [*so/neither* + **auxiliary/modal verb** + **subject**] as responses to statements with which the speaker agrees or to which the speaker assents. Such expressions are exemplified below.

So	**do**	I.
So	**does**	she.
Neither	**can**	we.
Neither	**has**	she.
So	**would**	they.
Neither	**did**	my brother.
So	**should**	you.
Neither	**was**	New York.
Neither	**will**	Jim.

4.9 The emphatic do

We have already seen how English speakers use the auxiliary verb *to do* for negation, the formation of questions, and the construction of other clauses in which the **verb** precedes the **subject**. However, the verb *to do* may also be used to emphasize the veracity of the statement being asserted by the speaker. By using *to do* as an **auxiliary verb** and placing it before the unconjugated main verb, the speaker emphasizes that his or her assertion is factually accurate. Speakers use this construction only when they wish to add great emphasis to the truth of the matter being asserted.

Note that the emphatic *do* can only be used in the simple present and simple past tenses. To add this same sort of emphasis to sentences with verbs in other tenses, English speakers use intonation to stress the auxiliary verb in question or intentionally fail to contract the auxiliary verb (e.g., *I* **will** *go to work tomorrow* or *He* **has** *been there before*).

TABLE 62. USING THE EMPHATIC *DO*

Normal declarative sentence	I know the President.
Emphatic declarative sentence	I really **do** know the President.
Normal declarative sentence	I went to the movies last night.
Emphatic declarative sentence	Yes! I **did** go to the movies last night.
Normal declarative sentence	My mother loves Mexican food.
Emphatic declarative sentence	No really! My mother **does** love Mexican food.
Normal declarative sentence	Kennedy defeated Nixon in 1960.
Emphatic declarative sentence	It's true! Kennedy **did** defeat Nixon in 1960!

INDEX OF TABLES

Part 1: Presenting English Verbs

Table 1. Summary of English verbal tense and aspect..21
Table 2. Conjugated forms of the verb *to do* 22
Table 3. Present simple of the verb *to go*...23
Table 4. Present, past, and future continuous of the verb *to go* 24
Table 5. Past simple of the verb *to go* 25
Table 6. Present perfect of the verb *to go*..25
Table 7. Past perfect of the verb *to go* 26
Table 8. Future simple of the verb *to go* 27
Table 9. Future perfect of the verb *to go* 27
Table 10. Present, past, and future perfect continuous of the verb *to go*.................28
Table 11. Irregular verb patterns...29
Table 12. Modal auxiliary verbs..34
Table 13. The first conditional 40
Table 14. The second conditional 41
Table 15. The third conditional 42
Table 16. The zero conditional 43
Table 17. Common verbs followed by gerunds and infinitives 46
Table 18. Contractions with pronouns and present tense forms of the verb *to be* 53
Table 19. Contractions with pronouns and present tense forms of the verb *to have* 54
Table 20. Contractions with pronouns and past tense forms of the verb *to have*............54
Table 21. Contractions with pronouns and the verb *will*..55
Table 22. Contractions with pronouns and the verb *would*.....................................55

Table 23. Contractions with present and past tense forms of the verb *to be* and *not* 57

Table 24. Contractions with auxiliary verbs and *not* 58

Part 2: Presenting English Nouns and Pronouns

Table 25. Pronunciation of the plural suffix –s/-es 64

Table 26. Nouns with irregular Germanic plural forms 65

Table 27. Nouns with irregular Latin or Greek plural forms................................66

Table 28. Count nouns and non-count nouns 70

Table 29. Examples of collective nouns 73

Table 30. Examples of pronoun subtypes 76

Table 31. Personal pronouns..78

Part 3: Presenting other Types of Words: Adjectives, Prepositions, and Adverbs

Table 32. Comparative and superlative forms of adjectives 86

Table 33. Examples of adjectives of one and two syllables whose comparatives and superlatives are formed with *more* and *most* due to phonotactic awkwardness 87

Table 34. Examples of adjectives of more than two syllables whose comparatives and superlatives are formed with *more* and *most* 88

Table 35. Irregular comparative and superlative forms of adjectives 89

Table 36. Present and past participles 92

Table 37. Preposition stranding in questions 98

Table 38. Preposition standing in declarative sentences 98

Table 39. Using the prepositions *in* and *on*..102

Table 40. Using the prepositions *to* and *toward*...103

Table 41. Adverbs derived from adjectives..106

Table 42. Adverbs that have the same form as adjectives..................................107

Table 43. Adverbs of manner 110

Table 44. Adverbs of frequency 110

Table 45. Adverbs of degree..111
Table 46. Adverbs of place...112
Table 47. Adverbs of time 112
Table 48. Clause-final adverbs 113
Table 49. Comparative and superlative forms of adverbs 116
Table 50. Commonly confused adverbs 118
Table 51. Using *no* and *not* 119

Part 4: Presenting English Syntax
Table 52. Forming *yes/no* questions with auxiliary verbs 125
Table 53. Forming *yes/no* questions with the verb *to be* 126
Table 54. Forming questions with negated auxiliary verbs...127
Table 55. Forming questions with wh-words 129
Table 56. Examples of question tags 133
Table 57. Using question tags 135
Table 58. Using the impersonal *it*...142
Table 59. Using the impersonal *there* 144
Table 60. Alternate method of forming the second conditional with subject-verb inversion 148
Table 61. Alternate method of forming the third conditional with subject-verb inversion 149
Table 62. Using the emphatic *do* 152

www.ingramcontent.com/pod-product-compliance
Lightning Source LLC
Chambersburg PA
CBHW041524220426
43670CB00002B/25